Dogs That Point, Fish That Bite

Dogs That Point,

Fish That Bite

Outdoor Essays by **Jim Dean**

The University of North Carolina Press

Chapel Hill & London

42704

The material contained
in this volume originally
appeared in *Wildlife in
North Carolina*, the magazine of the North Carolina
Wildlife Resources
Commission.

Manufactured in the
United States of America

The paper in this book
meets the guidelines for
permanence and durability
of the Committee on
Production Guidelines for
Book Longevity of the
Council on Library
Resources.

Library of Congress
Cataloging-in-Publication Data
Dean, Jim, 1940–
Dogs that point, fish that bite :
outdoor essays / by Jim Dean.
      p.   cm.
Essays originally published between
the years 1978–1995 in the
monthly column "Our natural
heritage" appearing in Wildlife in
North Carolina magazine.
ISBN 0-8078-2234-5 (cloth: alk.
paper)
1. Hunting — North Carolina —
Anecdotes.   2. Fishing — North
Carolina — Anecdotes   3. Outdoor
life — North Carolina — Anecdotes.
I. Title.
SK113.D435   1995
799'.09756 — dc20   95-13393
                              CIP

99 98 97 96 95   5 4 3 2 1

FOR MY MOTHER AND FATHER

Contents

Preface

The columns that appear here, gleaned from over seventeen years of writing about the outdoors in North Carolina, are organized into a loose chronicle of a sporting year, with a generous allowance for digressions. Since outdoor activity is often at an ebb the first three months of the year, it seemed appropriate to begin with the opening day of the trout season in April. That's when I have always celebrated the commencement of my "year" in the company of good friends and spring peepers on the banks of a trout stream just awakening from winter. And with the exception of late season bobwhite hunting, it winds down for me sometime between New Year's and the first wave of catalogs.

Although fishing and hunting provide the "glue," readers may decide that the real theme has more often been a celebration of our resources and traditions, tempered by the sad awareness of their steady retreat. Most of the places where I enjoyed fishing and hunting with my father, grandfather, and brothers forty years ago either no longer exist or have changed dramatically. In the Piedmont, fishing opportunities seem to be holding their own, but the future of hunting in much of this region is far less secure. I now drive past fifteen miles of strip malls where, just a few years ago, I walked fields behind dogs. Our family farm barely escaped becoming the site of a huge hazardous waste incinerator, but a tide of development threatens to make it an island.

The past twenty years have also seen vast changes in eastern North Carolina, not just on the Outer Banks but also in the fertile swamps, river bottoms, blackwater creeks, and sounds. When I wrote the first of these columns, Currituck's beaches were wild, and the Sound was not only regarded as the East Coast's prime waterfowling area; it also offered the finest brackish-water largemouth bass fishing in the world. That's a huge resource to lose in one bite, but it's not the only large chunk that's little more than a memory now. In the mountains, the changes may be less visible, but bulldozers are just beyond the ridge, and many favorite trout streams that were virtually pristine in the 1970s are threatened by acid rain and silted from logging and development. Anyone who has lived in North Carolina, or anywhere else for that matter, can make a long list of similar examples. Our last wild places are being mopped up, along with the small farms, rural traditions, and unregenerate citizens, customs, and habits that make us unique — and it is all happening in an eye-blink. Yet there still remain — for the moment, at least — opportunities to enjoy some of the things these columns celebrate. You simply have to know where to look, have the mind-set to appreciate what you find and, most especially, the good sense not to be too specific in telling people where you found it.

Even so, I hope that what appears in this collection will at least prove entertaining, especially for those who have shared similar experiences. Perhaps it will also become more obvious to folks who don't hunt and fish that those of us who include these activities among our outdoor pursuits are not altogether lacking in sensitivity or humor — that, in fact, we are frequently very serious conservationists and environmentalists whose love of wildlife and sporting traditions is founded in the knowledge that nature, for all its grace and beauty, is relentlessly unsentimental, has no regard whatever for the individual (including us), and is, as Alfred, Lord Tennyson, wrote, most assuredly "red in tooth and claw." I would argue that such a random design places all humans in the role of predator governed by the same laws that control the population of any animal, and our membership doesn't depend on whether we personally choose to consume wildlife directly or not. Like it or not, our very existence is consumptive in infinite ways — our lawns, our homes, our food, our cotton shirts, our petroleum-based plastics, our excrement, and even our embalmed bodies in cemetery plots. One could say that most human hunters at least understand their role and go to some trouble and expense to preserve habitat and enhance the populations of their prey. That humans can find pleasure or comfort — and perhaps, uniquely, any humor — in such a bleak and random arrangement doesn't let us off the hook, but it does suggest that we have evolved to become very special animals.

The chapters that make up this book were originally published in the magazine *Wildlife in North Carolina* as columns appearing each month on the inside front cover under the heading "Our Natural Heritage." The fifty columns in this collection were gleaned from nearly two hundred that have been published since the first one appeared in the January 1978 issue. Initially, the idea was that "Our Natural Heritage" would cover lesser-known aspects of North Carolina's history, particularly subjects related to our natural resources or events that had, in some way, shaped, changed, or defined our environment. After the first two years, however, the purely historical columns began to appear more sporadically as sources dried up. While remnants of this theme still exist in more recent columns — particularly in observations on our rapidly changing landscape and customs — the column has become more personal, covering the various pleasures, obsessions, frustrations, and often humorous aspects of fishing, hunting, and their related outdoor pursuits. Longtime readers of *Wildlife in North Carolina* would probably agree, how-ever, that the current themes remain consistent with the magazine's purpose. Now in its fifty-ninth year and sup-ported largely by paid subscriptions, the magazine is the official publication of the North Carolina Wildlife Re-sources Commission, the state agency charged with the conservation of all wildlife in the state and the regulation of hunting, trapping, inland fishing, and boating.

The idea of publishing a selection of "Our Natural Heritage" columns came up in casual conversation one summer afternoon in 1986, when I was fly fishing for largemouth bass on an old millpond with my longtime friend Matthew Hodgson, who was then director of the University of North Carolina Press. The Press had just entered into an agreement with the Wildlife Commission to publish a collection of some of the best features, photo-graphs, and artwork that had appeared in *Wildlife in North Carolina* during the past fifty years. Associate editor Law-rence S. Earley and I had already begun editing that book, and it was to be published in 1987 with the same title as the magazine. Matt told me that he was interested in pub-lishing another "sporting book" and said that he thought one might be buried among my columns. I was flattered, but I was not quite prepared to accept the possibility that I might have completed a book before it had ever occurred to me to write it. Besides, I wasn't convinced there was a market for used columns, especially since I had pitched my tent, subject-wise, in what was clearly becoming a polit-ically incorrect encampment. The truth was, however, that I felt I simply didn't have the spare time to devote to such a project.

The idea languished until just before Matt's retirement in 1993, when he encouraged David Perry, an editor at the UNC Press, to pin me down. David, who is also an avid fisherman, pointed out that the book was, indeed, essen-

tially finished, and that putting it together would in no
way infringe on my fishing time. Furthermore, he argued,
when published material piles up over the years until the
stack approximates the thickness of a book, only the author's better judgment or the aggressive indifference of
publishers can forestall the inevitable. Since the Press was
still interested, that left the ball in my court. That following summer, with the support of the Wildlife Commission,
I began to reread and edit the columns. I also discovered
that David, like all fishermen, had been less than candid
regarding the impact on my fishing.

A tremendous number of people have contributed in various ways to these columns. There is no way for me to
express my appreciation to them all, yet I cannot fail to
thank my friend and coworker, Larry Earley, who as associate editor of the magazine has edited these pieces since
the beginning. He and the magazine's assistant editor, Vic
Venters, have saved me from countless embarrassments.
A. Sidney Baynes, chief of the Wildlife Commission's Division of Conservation Education and my boss, not only
encouraged the publication of this collection but cleared
the way to make it happen. I also owe much to my other
fellow employees in the agency for their help over the
years. To Matt Hodgson and David Perry, I can truthfully
say that this book exists because of their confidence and
persistence.

It is even more difficult to recognize all the many
friends who have provided the fodder for these pieces, in-
tentionally or otherwise. I have been blessed with wonderful — and tolerant — companions whose good cheer, love
of tradition, and keen sense of the absurd have made so
many outings memorable. Mike Gaddis, Jack Avent, Andy
Aretakis, Joe McDade, Reid Bahnson, Alvin Johnson Jr.,
and many others have generously shared their skills. More

than that, they understand that true friendship is knowing when nothing need be said. I particularly miss my
oldest trout-fishing buddy and mentor A. J. Johnson (Alvin's father), who died in 1994 at the age of eighty-eight.
He enriched the lives of his many friends, and he will
always be with me when I'm knee-deep in trout water. And
certainly very similar feelings exist for my grandfather,
W. S. Dean, who died in 1968, and my father, William
Graham Dean. From the time I was eight years old, they
took me with them and made me part of grand adven-
tures. They inspired an enduring love of old millponds,
eastern blackwater rivers, bird dogs, beanfields, and duck
blinds. My other grandparents had no interest in hunting
or fishing, but growing up with them in Halifax and rural
Northampton Counties in the 1940s and 1950s helped
instill a respect for simple living.

For my dear mother, Margaret Geneva Brown Dean,
who died in 1992, I can only say "Here it is, and I'm
sad you didn't get to see it finished." More than anyone,
she and Dad sacrificed in ways my brothers, Graham and
John, and I will never fully know. Finally, I have been
blessed with the two very best companions a father could
hope to have outdoors or anywhere else — my children,
Scott and Susan.

It should be obvious to anyone who reads this book that
I have managed to have a heap of fun most of my life, and
especially those times I've spent outdoors during the
nearly five decades since my grandfather and I watched
my first new cork slide beneath the dark waters of Bluegill
Pond. I sincerely hope you have been fortunate enough to
have similar memories, and good friends and family to
share them.

Just Once a Year

There aren't many certainties in life, but I think I can come close with one prediction. Although I may not know where I'm going to eat lunch tomorrow, I've got a pretty good idea where I'll be the first Saturday of each April for the rest of my life. In case you haven't already figured it out, that's the traditional opening day of the trout season in North Carolina.

For me, the anticipation of opening day begins in early January when I am swept westward into the high Appalachians on a tide of fishing tackle catalogs to a primitive cabin that overlooks a stream flush with wild trout. I will make these mental scouting trips for three long, dreaming months. Then one gray day like all the others, when I have not been paying close enough attention to separate veri- from -similitude, I will find that I am actually bouncing along in my four-wheel-drive truck. Rod tubes are rattling against fly boxes, nets, and other gear in the back, and I am passing bright splashes of forsythia as I drive out of another winter.

A. J. Johnson and his son Alvin and I like to arrive early to freshen the mouse poison and open the curtains to let in the slanting, dust-flecked shafts of pale sun. Friends begin to arrive in late afternoon, and the traditional oyster stew will be cooked on the woodstove in a kitchen as hot as a nursing home. A. J. will add a bit of crumbled red pepper to the stew, invariably a bit more than would have been prudent. Well, why not? It's his cabin and his stew.

After months of following a rigid schedule, there will suddenly be time for whimsy, time to walk out on the porch with a steaming cup of coffee or wander up the dirt road beside the stream. The stream will be high with runoff, and the rush of water full of promise. I suspect every angler mentally fishes such water, picking out likely spots where a trout might be holding in the icy current. It may be the best fishing of the weekend, and you savor it in a twilight welcomed by the ancient chorus of spring peepers.

Of course, opening day is largely a ritualistic celebration, and trout seldom play a major role. The streams are often crowded, the trout recalcitrant, and the weather raw. I have more often fished in a cold drizzle than in bright sun, and at least two opening days were accompanied by snow flurries. But there was also the spring of 1978, which followed one of the most bitter winters in recent North Carolina memory. The early afternoon temperature that opening day climbed to an incredible 88 degrees. In stretches of the stream that had not been disturbed by earlier anglers, wild browns and rainbows leaped at our dry flies and chased nymphs halfway across the gold and emerald pools.

There was also a cool, overcast day that bathed the leafless mountains in silver fog, and every twig and pine needle was tipped with a diamond droplet. That morning, a dark shape appeared behind the dry fly as it floated on the current. The fly began to drag, and then it sank, yet the dark shape still drifted beneath it. No trout would eat such a clumsy offering, but there was an improbable flash of white — a mouth opening — and the fly was gone. Moments later, nineteen inches of quivering brown trout lay in the net. Released, it swam slowly back into the shadows — a wild fish almost too large to believe in such a small public stream. A ghost, perhaps, or a dream? Surely no one would believe it that evening, and I was not certain I would even risk sharing it. But, of course, I did.

Such moments are so rare on opening day that I have

learned to approach this time of renewal with no expectations. Indeed, one year we decided not to fish. The day dawned in torrents of rain, and the roads were filled with torrents of trucks and cars full of wet, grim-faced fishermen.

"We'll just sit beside the fire today," we said. "Drink coffee, eat a huge breakfast. Tie a few flies and shoot the bull. Let the mobs pound the water and freeze. We'll go tomorrow after they've all got pneumonia."

Late that afternoon, the rain slackened, and we decided to drive up to a local trout pond and watch the circus. You've seen the photos of opening-day fishermen standing elbow to elbow, fully encircling a pond that contains a tight knot of thoroughly spooked trout. Add a cold rain to that scene, and you have a fair representation of what we found when we arrived.

We sat in the car, toasty and comfortable, observing the hordes. They looked miserable. It cheered us immensely. After a few minutes, someone caught a small trout. We fell silent.

"What do you think?" someone asked tentatively.

"We've got our gear," came an answer. "Wouldn't hurt to try it a few minutes."

There was little conversation on the way back to the cabin two hours later. The car heater that had seemed so warm earlier poured out a steady rush of arctic air. We were wet from head to foot from leaky rain jackets and waders. Our gear lay in a sodden mass in the trunk. No one had caught a trout.

"We almost m-m-made it," someone finally said.

Children of the Moon

"The child is father of the man," wrote William Wordsworth in the opening line of his ode "Intimations of Immortality." Some would say that explains a lot of shortcomings, though perhaps not nearly enough. Indeed, Mr. Wordsworth was obviously well acquainted with childlike adults long before the term "arrested development" became fashionable.

Some of us don't, you know. Grow up, that is. I myself have had some practical experience in the arena of extended childhood, and I've found that it becomes most noticeable each May as the full moon appears in the balmy night sky. That bright and perfect orb mysteriously drives billions of fat bluegills and shellcrackers to their spawning beds with the urge to beget while the begetting is good. The prospect strips the years from ancient anglers and makes us crazy. It is, after all, no coincidence that the word "lunacy" is derived from "lunar."

Like many moonstruck anglers, my longtime panfishing buddy and I indulge certain traditions during this once-a-year rite. It is, for example, essential that Jack Avent and I make this particular passage in his 1956 Granny Smith apple green Ford truck. Even without the '57 Thunderbird V-8 — three two-barrels, dual steel-packs, and flames painted under the hood — this is the perfect chariot to transport a pair of senescent, perch-jerking partners back to the future.

We load the rear bed with a wooden pond boat, a forty-eight-quart cooler, a couple of cricket cages, and enough rods and cane poles to stock a Kmart. We also carry a few light snacks just in case we get hungry, but no more than will fit into a second forty-eight-quart cooler and three or four paper sacks. There is no truth to the rumor that Jack once carried a whole Smithfield ham and an angel food cake.

The first stop is always at the same tackle shop we've frequented for years, and the banter is always the same. "Fill 'em up with insects," says Jack, setting the cages on the counter. "High test. We want maximum chirps per gallon."

We negotiate the last mile of a dirt path and launch the boat in the pond. The truck is filled with the sound of crickets singing boldly in the face of doom, and we join them: "Give us some crickets who are stout-hearted . . ."

Tradition calls for a light cane pole about fourteen to sixteen feet long, a sliding cork, and a couple of small split shot pinched on the line above a No. 8 or 10 hook. If you don't have a truck, the proper way to carry cane poles is sticking out a rear window, where they thumb their noses at any passing motorist who isn't fortunate enough to be going fishing.

Once the boat is launched and loaded with our tackle and provisions, the biggest problem is finding room to sit. But we manage, and with decent weather and any luck at all, the fishing is always good. We seek the larger spawning areas, looking for the countless circular depressions fanned out by the fish. They are often easy to spot along the banks or on shallow flats, and we can smell those too deep to see. As the action slows in one area, we move to another, baiting hooks with the same musty, unwashed hands that hold our sandwiches. The lemonade level falls; the cooler fills.

Late in the afternoon, slathered in suntan lotion and insect repellent, we drift contentedly under the warm sun, listening to the slap of water on the hull and the rasp of red-winged blackbirds. Stretched out with hands behind our heads and feet dangling in the water, we watch puffy cumulus clouds that invariably form the shapes of chickens. (Why is that, anyway? Is some obscure science at work here?)

For once, no one is thinking about deadlines and quotas. It is simple and timeless fishing that tends to blur memory so that you cannot be sure if it was four years ago that you caught a twenty-six-ounce bluegill, or twenty-six years ago that you caught a four-ounce bluegill.

I don't know what Jack thinks about, but I am often transported to identical days forty years earlier when my father or grandfather and I drifted across old millponds under shaggy cypress. Once again I am ten years old, lean and brown as a berry, and there is hair on my head. I have my wonderful bobber that whistles when a bream bites, and my hands smell like worms. The immortal redwings sing to me, and there is no intimation that this will ever end.

On the way home, Jack and I tune in an oldies station and listen to the songs of our youth over the invigorating growl of the exhausts. Roy Hamilton, Johnny Ace, and Bobby Blue Bland join the chirps of the surviving crickets.

A new 300ZX turbo pulls alongside us at a stoplight, and the driver glances over and revs the engine, confidently issuing an age-old challenge. His last incredulous, open-mouthed look at this rumbling ghost from the 1950s is of the rear end of a boat full of bluegills, poles, and flapping corks nestled between two swiftly disappearing taillights.

"Don't mess with the forever young," Jack says. Shirley and Lee are singing "Let the Good Times Roll." We do.

One Berry Picker Moves On

The berry picker is gone. No one has seen him since last winter, and the official story is that he packed up and left when the weather turned cold. Not that he will be missed.

The berry picker showed up two years ago in this small, isolated mountain settlement and quickly earned his nickname. Almost every day, he walked the dirt road carrying a sack. Occasionally he could be seen cutting through backyards, and he seemed to pick times when his neighbors were away or indoors. He never came to the store, and he seldom spoke to anyone even when greeted. People thought that was strange, even for a Yankee.

First the cherries disappeared from the lower limbs of a tree alongside the road. Then, the tomatoes never seemed to get quite ripe, and sweet corn became a rare commodity. Stacks of firewood dwindled just a bit faster than you'd reckon they should. Full kerosene drums echoed when you thumped them. After a new charcoal grill and a lawn mower evaporated, people moved their porch furniture indoors.

Everyone knew who it was, of course. Like any newcomer, he'd been a natural object of suspicion even before the first tomato disappeared. He only thought he wasn't being watched. Besides, it wasn't exactly circumstantial evidence when he'd leave his cabin with an empty poke and complete his rounds with a full one.

From my viewpoint, the situation began to get serious when Joe reported that he'd confronted the berry picker sneaking through the rhododendron down on the creek early one morning with a string of trout. "I mentioned our little community agreement concerning trout and what we kept and what we didn't," said Joe, who is generally listened to when he mentions anything. "You never heard such cussing in your life. Said them trout were put there for him by the Almighty."

That explained why private vegetables and personal firewood were consistently falling into the public domain, but it didn't render an immediate solution. Neither Joe nor Claude nor anyone else, including me, felt that a few trout were worth it. Meanwhile, if the Almighty wasn't getting weary of His needful charge, those who were planting on His behalf surely were.

The truth is that the berry picker was pushing his luck more than he knew in this nineteenth-century village, where one of his neighbors was reputedly a reformed bootlegger, and another was reputedly not (reformed, that is). He also hadn't taken into account the rumor that another neighbor long gentled by these harsh hills and true friends had once served time for multiple murder. Nor, obviously, had the berry picker tried to remove any of the Almighty's trout from the private tributary across the ridge, where a caretaker regularly overlooked the domain with a can of Schaeffer in one hand and a .45 in the other.

And so the growing season passed in fretful tranquility. The summer people came and went, but the right opportunity and the means to seize it remained elusive.

Everyone agreed that we needed a man like Johnson. It was the near-legendary Johnson who years earlier had put the fear of God in the frogman, a tourist who had kept everyone awake at night for weeks shooting bullfrogs in puddles along the road until he made the mistake of jumping a frog on Johnson's claim. It was also Johnson who had once run into a couple of trout poachers up in the refuge and informed them they were breaking the law. At first they were not impressed.

"I saw your Jeep parked a forty-minute walk straight up the ridge," Johnson told them, "and my Bronco is parked five minutes down the creek. I don't think there's any way in the world you can beat me to your Jeep, but you damn well better try."

"That's the meanest man we ever met," the exhausted poachers told everyone at the store when they finally rolled in on the rims and stopped to try to buy four inner-tubes. "If we get out from in here, you tell him we ain't coming back."

But Johnson no longer visited regularly, and the berry picking situation was at an impasse when I closed up the cabin late last fall. On my first trip back this spring, I noticed that the furniture was back on the porches.

"What happened to the berry picker?" I asked at the store. "He didn't chance upon any mash barrels or walk into a bullet, did he?"

"Why, he just upped and left," said Joe, with a knowing smile on his face.

"Well, I'm glad to hear that," I said. "Maybe I'll be able to catch a trout and eat a tomato this year."

"I wouldn't count on that too heavily," sighed Claude. "There will always be a berry picker, you know, just not that particular one."

I was nearly out the door when a thought occurred to me. "Johnson didn't by chance get up here this past winter, did he?"

"Once, briefly. He asked how come his kerosene drum was empty. Could be somebody told him the Almighty was cold."

Fishing with Grandfathers

A year or two before my grandfather W. S. Dean died, he told me, "If anything happens to me, I want you to go into the garage and get my tackle box, rods, and any other fishing gear you want. It will be hectic around here for a few days when I pass on, and I don't want those things to get misplaced or be given away to someone else."

After he died, I kept his gear pretty much in the same condition as I'd found it. I used the paddles, but for years I kept the rest intact as a sort of memorial to the many good times we'd shared. I really didn't have much reason to want to use the split cane or old steel casting rods anyway. The steel rods were rusty, and the cane rod had been broken and crudely spliced at some time in the distant past. Until recently, I didn't even use Grandfather's fine old aluminum tackle box, although it was better than mine.

A few months ago, on a rainy afternoon, I decided to look through the old box, and as I had anticipated, it was a nostalgic trip. The box had always had a wonderful smell — a mixture of 6-12 insect repellent, reel oil, fly-line dressing, and five-cent cigars. Among the tins of hooks and familiar corks, I found the crippled minnow that Grandfather had been using the day we stalked the big one.

We had located a sizeable bass next to a brush pile in the millpond we usually fished. Grandfather had missed the strike that day, but our return engagement a week later had been planned as carefully as the invasion of

Normandy. That evening, we quietly loaded the boat and rowed across the pond. We even began whispering when we were within range. Grandfather cast the crippled minnow to an opening alongside the brush, and a huge bass engulfed it.

I suppose we weighed the fish before we released it, but I don't recall what it weighed and that's just as well. On a soggy afternoon years later, such details are unimportant. As I sat idly spinning the handle on my grandfather's old Pfleuger Supreme and recalling the many fishing trips we'd taken, I realized how much bass fishing has changed.

Back then, Grandfather had fished in a coat and tie instead of a jumpsuit, and the only patches he wore were the ones my grandmother sewed on the elbows. Those steel and bamboo rods have been replaced by graphite and boron, and the old knuckle-busting reels have given way to free-spool, magnetic antibacklash marvels. The crippled minnows and Oriental wigglers have been supplanted by a host of modern spinnerbaits, crankbaits, and plastic worms.

Even the fishing vehicles have changed. There's a world of difference between a four-wheel-drive truck and an ancient blue Buick with cane poles sticking out the rear window. The biggest changes have probably taken place in the boats used by bass fishermen. Today's bass boats are likely to cost as much as an automobile and are fully equipped with a powerful outboard, a foot-controlled electric motor, live wells, a depth finder, carpet, pedestal seats, and a host of other features.

I'm sure there are fishermen who long for the good old days and wish they'd never seen a bass boat or a depth finder, but I don't entirely agree. It's true that I still like to fish ponds and small lakes in much the same fashion as I did years ago, but I also prefer most modern fishing tackle to the gear it replaced. The new reels are far superior, and the same goes for rods. Many of the new lures are also better than the old ones, although I'll admit some of those old-time baits were outstanding.

As for bass boats, they've caught the brunt of a lot of unfair criticism, mostly from those who don't realize that these boats are among the safest, most comfortable, and most efficient fishing boats ever built. I suspect the real reason some of us long for the good old days and poke fun at modern angling technology is simply that there are so many more fishermen today, especially on large lakes.

Yet there is nothing to keep us from seeking our solitude on countless smaller lakes and thousands of ponds. At such spots, we can choose to toss a traditional deer-hair bass bug with a thoroughly modern graphite fly rod and get the best of both worlds. And when we fish the larger bodies of water in a modern bass boat, we can still maintain age-old traditions and practice the angling ethics that perpetuate our sport. After all, someday these will be the good old days.

As for me, I've brought my grandfather's tackle box out of retirement to help me bridge the gap. Among the modern plugs, plastic worms, and high-tech reels, you can still find a pack of my grandfather's cigars and a few other mementos. I think he'd like that. And that old tackle box smells just as good as it ever did.

Fishing for Ice Age Trout

As I begin writing this column, it appears that I'll be finishing it around midnight. In a day of wrapping up odds and ends before a vacation, it was one of the odds that didn't get ended. Shortly before daylight in the morning, my son Scott and I will drop this off at the office and head west. Five hours later, I'll take off my watch and put it in the glove compartment. Then I'll turn up the single-lane dirt road that climbs over what locals call the Staircase. When we drop into the valley on the far side, we'll be home.

I've been coming to these remote mountains for many years to fish for trout, explore the ancient trails, and taste a sense of history. In some parts of these hills, you can move in and out of the last century simply by taking the right road, entering an old church, or buying a Cheerwine in a village grocery.

The tiny cabin I stay in was built out of timbers strewn down the gorge by the 1916 floods. The furniture—a bed, a chair, and a table—was made by Bill Crump, who built what he and his neighbors needed with a water-driven saw. If you wanted a bedroom suite, you brought him a picture out of Sears & Roebuck and he'd start looking for the right tree to cut. Resting on the rafters of his shop was a handsome walnut coffin he made for himself years before he died—kept his likker in it, they said. He died in the 1960s, and his abandoned house fell in twenty years later. Last year, Scott and I found what was left of his straight-8 Buick rusting away in a thick clump of rhododendron. Today, it's hard to imagine how he ever got it up the steep trail to the Forest Service road.

I guess I don't need to tell you that I love this part of the state, and I have spent my share of spare time fishing its trout streams. Years ago, in that first flush of discovery when the soul is possessed by salmonoids, my fellow anglers and I would leave Raleigh in the middle of the night, arrive at dawn, and fish until dark, then drive five hours back home and work the next day. There was literally no price we wouldn't pay for an hour on a trout stream, and that kind of obsession is so rich and wonderful that you feel obliged to try to share it with your children.

Of course, you can't really transfer an obsession, and especially not from parent to child. There is a natural barrier that seems to ensure that few, if any, offspring will acquire the identical interests of their fathers and mothers. Indeed, children are far more likely to gravitate to an opposite extreme, perhaps driven only to express their own identity. Given that general rule, you'd probably expect any offspring of mine to be mathematicians living in metropolitan penthouses and reading only fashion magazines and *TV Guide*.

Actually, in a selfish way, I've been luckier than most. My kids have their own obsessions — which is as it should be — but they also like to share mine.

So it is that this afternoon Scott and I will park the car, string up our fly rods, and stick peanut butter and jelly sandwiches in our vests. Then we'll begin to walk. The first mile along this particular creek has a fading trail, but above the falls, the trail peters out and you have to stay in the creek or climb high up the steep banks to the ridgeline above the thick laurel "hells" to find enough room to walk.

We'll worry about the lack of a trail later. Meanwhile, we'll begin to fish this tiny tributary above the falls and stay in the creek until it's little more than a trickle. We may catch twenty to thirty trout apiece, but it's unlikely that any will be longer than eight inches.

These are brook trout, remnants of the ice ages, and the only native game fish in these remote headwaters. The brown and rainbow trout are both latecomers, first stocked in North Carolina streams in the late 1800s. Indeed, the native brookie is actually a char rather than a trout.

That alone makes them special, but there is more to it than that. These trout can exist only in the purest environment where water temperatures average 55 to 65 degrees Fahrenheit. Today such conditions exist largely in the small headwaters of some — not all — streams. Thus, to me the brook trout is yet another link with this region's history — clinging somewhat precariously to an existence that seems too fragile to last.

For Scott and me, fishing this kind of water is at least as much ritual as it is pure fun. The fish are tiny jewels of dark mottled green with pale blue spots touched lightly in the center with scarlet. Their fins are flags of black, red, and white. Getting to these fish is the only difficult part. Catching them is easy, and they're also good to eat, although we never keep any.

In a wistful way, all of this is connected. It is the pleasure of fishing with a son, the sharing of history, and the visceral gratification of using a skill. But it is also the satisfaction of knowing that an appreciation for all of this is being passed to at least one more generation. It is, after all, the only protection any of us can provide for the things we have cared about.

If our children do not have an opportunity to learn the value of such things, they will have no incentive to protect them and pass them on to their own children. It may be the best inheritance we can leave, and having said that, I'm on my way west.

Calendar Art and the Sacrificial Bass

The trouble with an obsession is that reality rarely seems to live up to the dream. Take bass fishing, for example. In the mind of the obsessed angler, the quintessence of the sport is probably best exemplified by calendar art out of the 1940s or 1950s. You know the kind of painting I'm talking about. Here is a handsome gentleman, graying a bit in the moustache, but still robust and fully capable of handling the oars of the skiff he's sitting in. Clutched rakishly in his teeth is a pipe, and on his head is a jaunty fedora bespangled with lures and flies.

Of course, you only notice this after you have looked past the gigantic largemouth bass that is leaping in a shower of spray amid a tangle of lily pads. Naturally, there's a Lucky 13 (always in frog finish) poking out of its mouth like a stogie. The sky is blue, the angler is smiling, the rod is bent, and all's right with the world.

That image — or something similar — is what drives those of us who have bitten hard on the treble hooks of bass fishing. There is, by the way, a myth that only fish are ever hooked. Anglers can also taste the steel, and unlike some bass, once anglers are solidly hooked they are never set free again.

All winter, the bass fisherman works on his tackle, buys new gear, reads books on *Micropterus salmoides,* and dreams his dreams. This past winter, I seemed to have a particularly bad case of cabin fever, and I spent many evenings "getting ready." I rearranged tackle boxes, replaced line, sharpened hooks, repainted old lures. It's been years since I awaited the arrival of spring with such delicious tension, and I was ready to sally forth at the first opportunity. This year, life would duplicate art — calendar art, at least.

I suppose you know what happened. For over two months, everything went wrong. Plans fell through, equipment failed, partners reneged, work conflicted, and the weeks sailed by. Worse than that, the occasional trips I managed were unsatisfactory. Instead of lunkers leaping in lily pads, I had to be content with an occasional yearling yanked out of some stagnant water hole.

"What's the point?" a nonfishing friend responded when I complained about my frustration. "Why do you torture yourself? You devote all that imagination and energy to fish — not to mention money and time — and you readily admit that you haven't had a single truly successful trip this spring. I think you're crazy."

Well, yes. And until that late Sunday afternoon in May, I'll admit that I was beginning to think there might be more personal satisfaction in something like, say, golf. Sooner or later you're going to get the ball in the hole. No such certainty exists in fishing.

But as I said, there was that Sunday afternoon when I decided to visit a small one-acre pond that I hadn't fished in awhile. The pond is nearly forty years old, and it certainly looks fishy, with all the old stumps, arrowroot, and cattails that threaten to choke it. Of course, the fishier a pond looks, the poorer the fishing is, as a rule. But what the heck, I figured, I could at least enjoy the fading hours of a fine day in the company of red-winged blackbirds and frogs. I've done worse.

I decided to fish with a fly rod and deer-hair bug simply because if I'm not going to catch fish, I'd rather be skunked on my own terms. At least it's fun to cast and work a bug.

Imagine my surprise at catching a bass. Then another,

and another. The fourth one weighed three pounds, certainly a satisfying fish on a fly rod. Finally, at dusk, I made a long cast toward a stump and twitched the bug. The strike was immediate and furious, and I was looking at five pounds of largemouth cartwheeling over the dark water. The bass jumped clear of the water three times, twice ran the line into the backing, and generally towed me around the pond. The whole thing seemed to occur in slow motion, and I was distinctly aware of the way the slanting light reflected off the droplets of water and shone through the transparent fins each time the bass jumped.

When I finally landed the fish, I debated whether to take a picture of it, but somehow it seemed more appropriate simply to commit this one to memory. I weighed the fish, held it in the water for a few minutes, then turned it loose.

Behavioral scientists would call this reinforcement, like feeding a laboratory rat to reward it for some simple act. Once lab rats are conditioned, it takes only an occasional feeding to keep them performing. I'll buy that.

Somewhere behind the Post Office

Call some place paradise;
Kiss it goodbye.
—from "The Last Resort," by The Eagles

A fellow angler recently transplanted to western North Carolina has written to complain. "I love to fish for trout, but none of the local fishermen will direct me to the best spots," he lamented. "One fellow suggested I try the stream behind the post office, but he couldn't recall the name of it. Do you know of a stream around here that flows behind a post office?"

Indeed I do, I responded. I'm well acquainted with that stream, as well as a number of other phantom ponds, streams, and lakes apparently located behind post offices around the globe. Every super fishing spot lies ("lie" being the operative word here) behind some post office. Anyone who gives you such directions will never be able to recall the name of the spot, or its exact distance from the back step of the postal facility — assuming, of course, that you began your journey from the right P.O.

Before you get riled at such a provincial attitude, it might be worthwhile to analyze the motivation. First, I should explain that my sentiments are with the close-mouthed mountaineers. On the surface, this reluctance seems selfish, but so what? It's also based on sad experience. After all, we may not know how many angels can dance on a pinhead, but it's not difficult to figure out how many anglers it takes to overcrowd a tiny stream.

With more and more people sharing our dwindling natural areas, the days are fast disappearing when hunters or fishermen can pursue their sport in relative solitude, and if you find a spot you especially like, you're foolish to blab about it. We learn to protect our interests.

In the early 1970s, with the help of some maps and a lot of foot-weary hiking through a public area that had no trails, I located a fine stretch of remote brook trout water. For over a decade, I fished that water fairly regularly and never encountered another angler. Then, in a moment of amiable weakness, one day I happened to mention it to someone. He began to fish there, and later he took several friends. I stopped going when that wilderness creek began to attract more traffic than the Intracoastal Waterway.

I blame no one but myself, even though I realize that some of the fishing pressure may have been entirely coincidental. It's not, however, a mistake I'll make again.

As I noted earlier, this isn't simply selfishness. You can make a pretty good case for secrecy on purely environmental grounds. Some years ago, when wild turkey restoration efforts were beginning to pay off, a news article appeared just prior to the spring gobbler season. The gist of it was that a particular spot — not a very large one, either — was touted as the most likely place in the state to bag a gobbler. Of course, you know what happened. When opening day arrived, crowds flocked to the area, and nobody was glad to see anybody else.

Fortunately, turkeys are very wary creatures, and the restoration effort suffered no setback. But the incident demonstrated the potential for publicity to pose a risk to wildlife resources in some small, fragile, or sensitive areas.

Was the brook trout fishery hurt by the growing pressure in that tiny stream I fished? Hard to say. I didn't keep any of the fish I caught, but if other anglers kept too many fish, the population could have been hurt. Brook trout are easy to catch, and there are instances where populations of these native trout have been virtually eliminated.

Not many years ago, it was routine for various agencies and publications to furnish highly detailed "where to go" information. Sometimes we were even told the exact spot to fish or hunt; which rock to stand on; which tree to hide behind. This kind of reporting is increasingly rare, however, and that's almost surely a good thing. Perhaps it's because more and more folks recognize the potential threat that publicity poses to resources.

It's also why many of us keep our favorite spots "behind the post office." If people are serious about their sport and take the time to search out their own secret spots, they're far less likely to harm those resources. They've earned their solitude, and you can't blame them for clinging to it.

Let the Good Earth Roll

Jack Avent and I were fishing the large bed of lily pads so intently that at first we didn't notice the man and his wife. They were sitting on a dock on the opposite side of the small cove.

"You ain't going to catch anything today," the man said as we reached the end of the lilies near the dock. There was a slight edge to his voice — not exactly unfriendly, but with a hint of challenge,. as though he were daring us to disagree.

"Well, maybe a couple of little ones will make a mistake," Jack hedged. Actually, we'd already landed seven or eight bass farther down the lake, but we learned long ago that it's never a good idea to encourage potential competition.

"Won't happen," said the man. "Fish never bite when the earth's rolling."

"You're right, it's a bit windy, but we've had pretty good —" Jack began before the man cut him off.

"It ain't wind," said the man, his eyes flashing. He seemed truly offended that Jack wasn't in complete and immediate agreement. "Any fool can tell the earth is rolling today. Fish know it. You ain't gonna catch nothing. Earth's rolling. Look at it. It's rolling, all right."

Jack didn't answer, but he looked at me, one eyebrow slightly raised. I pictured the earth spinning easily on its axis like a giant top until the tip of Antarctica hit a knothole on the cosmic floor and the whole orb began to wobble wildly. I was willing to concede that fish and fools might notice such a thing.

Jack backed the boat up so that we could fish the lilies again. "You suppose he's had a few snorts, or is he serious?" he half-whispered. "I thought I'd heard every excuse in the book, but I believe I'd give a twenty-dollar bill to catch a bass in front of that guy."

Jack's money was safe, unfortunately, but that's luck for you. Or maybe it's just hard to make an accurate cast when your planet is on a toot. As we left the cove, I glanced over my shoulder at the man. He'd given up on us and was jawing at his wife. She looked as though she had a working familiarity with his theory.

Fishermen are infamous for excuses, some more seriously ventured than others. When I was a kid, my grandfather would explain that I wouldn't catch fish unless I "held my mouth right." The twinkle in his eyes gave it away, but I'd try several different mouth-holds anyway. No need to take any chances. In fact, I think I had his advice in mind when I smoked my first cigar years later. Maybe the right way to hold your mouth was to clamp it around a stogie. After all, Grandpa had smoked cheap cigars, and he'd caught fish when I hadn't. Didn't work for me, by the way.

Over the years, I have tried to remember all the whimsical reasons I've heard that attempt to explain why fish don't bite. "I used to hear you couldn't catch fish if you put the worm on the hook backwards," said Jack. My long-time ocean pier–fishing buddy, Pete Leo, explains that you have to call fish. We always laughed, but after he'd catch half a dozen, you could hear grown men up and down the pier chanting, "Here fishy, here fishy."

Like folk remedies, some of these superstitions and homespun beliefs seem to have merit. Surely you've heard this old rhyme:

When the wind's in the East, fish bite least;
When the wind's in the West, fish bite best;

> When the wind's in the South, it blows the bait
> Into the fish's mouth.

I used to think this was pure foolishness, but now I'm not so sure. On freshwater lakes and ponds in North Carolina, at least, winds out of the west or southwest usually accompany relatively stable weather, and that's often better for fishing. On the other hand, a sharp cold front or a northeaster almost invariably creates a day or two of poor fishing. Prevailing wind direction is connected to weather patterns, barometric pressure, and other meteorological influences that really do affect fishing.

And what about Solunar Tables? The influence of the moon on tides is well known, but do moon phases really affect fishing? Try to convince a bluegill fisherman that the moon doesn't influence spawning and fishing success. I've been a doubter, but I honestly don't know.

Even so, I'd be careful how much trust I put in calendars that have those little fish symbols that are supposed to indicate when the fishing is good. I'm not calling any names, but I once asked a calendar designer how she knew which days were good. "Oh, I don't," she said. "I just stick 'em on anywhere."

The best advice I know in these matters is quite simple. When you can arrange your affairs to go fishing, forget all the signs, homilies, advice, and folklore. Just go. But while you're out there, you might want to hold your mouth right.

Getting Lost and Loving It

.The last time I got lost, it was on the off-ramp of a giant cloverleaf where I pulled out of bumper-to-bumper traffic with my emergency lights blinking and sat studying a map while considerate drivers honked their horns and gave me hand signals to show their sympathy. I eventually had to ask directions before I was comfortably assured that I was on the right path again. This particular brand of lost happens to me so often that I no longer measure distance in miles, but in "asks." It's far more accurate. For example, Pennsylvania's limestone trout streams are only four asks from Raleigh, but I've had some six-ask trips just getting across town.

Being lost in the woods is quite a different matter. For one thing, it's nowhere near as dangerous, and there's no one around to share in your wonderment. Indeed, I've come to cherish my considerable ability to lose my bearings. These days, with wilderness drying up everywhere, the feeling of not quite knowing where you are in the woods is rather pleasurable, at least at the outset. I tend to hold with Robert Ruark, who said, "If you don't care where you are, you ain't lost."

If that fails to assuage any apprehension, it's helpful to recall that Daniel Boone denied that he was ever truly lost, commenting only that he was once "a mite confused for six weeks."

The truth is that I have been lost in the classic sense only once that I recall. I had hiked a faint and unfamiliar three-mile trail into a remote trout stream in western North Carolina. Upon reaching the creek, I stopped to familiarize myself with the rock patterns, then hiked down-stream a mile or two. I planned to fish back to that spot, then climb the trail to the car.

I tend to get a bit engrossed when I'm fishing — imagine that — and as luck would have it, I fished well past my stopping place. Shortly after sunset, I quit fishing, thinking that the trail was still upstream. After a twenty-minute hike, I figured I must have walked past the trail without recognizing it. I turned around and walked briskly for thirty minutes without seeing anything familiar — or rather without seeing anything unfamiliar.

By the time it was dusk, I had pretty much tromped out a mile of new trail up and down the creek. Ruark notwithstanding, I was beginning to care where I was. At that point, I did what I should have done to begin with. I sat down and gave the matter some thought. I still wasn't convinced that I had fished past the trail, but the up-stream route seemed a poor bet. I knew that by heading downstream I would either pass the trail and recognize it or eventually reach some form of civilization between me and the Atlantic Ocean. If I wasn't out by full dark, I'd simply make camp and spend the night. It was too dangerous to walk those rhododendron slicks and outcrops at night. I was already recalling my Boy Scout handbook's instructions for making friction fires, lean-tos, and beds of hemlock when I crossed the trail a scant few yards from where I'd been sitting. I was almost disappointed.

Since that time, I've carried a simple survival kit when fishing or hunting. Having it is good insurance and gives me a sense of self-sufficiency. Of course, no one wants to lug ten pounds of insurance all day, but if you consider what you can't live without, you can make do with far less.

My survival kit includes a folding jackknife, a disposable butane lighter, and a small penlight — all lightweight items I'm likely to use anyway. In addition, I carry a disposable plastic blaze-orange poncho that folds up to about the size of a pack of cigarettes. It will provide some warmth and shelter, and it's also visible to searchers — an important feature if you happen to break an ankle. One of those thin space-age tarps with reflecting Mylar on one side would provide more warmth and protection, but it's a bit heavier. I also carry a police whistle. There's a limit to how long and loud you can holler if you're lost or hurt.

Some might want more first-aid items, a snakebite kit, water purification tablets, a couple of granola bars, bouillon cubes, waterproof matches, or a compass, but you've got to cut weight somewhere, so I add these items only when I think I might need them. You've already got hooks or bullets in case you need to roast a trout or a starling.

I almost forgot the most important thing — a small Ziplock bag of coffee. Your pot is the empty drink can leftover from lunch.

I figure if I spend the night out there, I'm certainly not going to deprive myself of a hot cup of Colombian the next morning. Who knows? My rescuers may bring a newspaper.

Death of a Turtle

Waves of heat rose from the white gravel that covered the railroad bed, and hot tar oozed from the ties. Ahead, the rails curved and disappeared around a bend. Just down the embankment to the right lay the river, an artery of 58-degree water that ran parallel to the tracks baking in the late summer sun.

Something caught my eye. A large male box turtle moved feebly on the gravel, trying to climb over the smooth, hot steel. How long had he been trapped between those rails, and how had he gotten there? I carried him into the thick undergrowth and left him in a moist, shaded spot. Maybe he would live.

Back on the tracks, I followed the curve for another two hundred yards looking for the path to the river, where I planned to fish. In that short distance, I found four other box turtles, all trapped between the rails. All dead.

After taking a closer look, it was easy to see how the turtles had become trapped. Here and there were small openings under the rails where the turtles, seeking the warmth of the gravel and ties, had crawled through. Once between the rails, they could not find the openings again, and eventually they perished in the heat. A more effective death trap could hardly be devised. If that many turtles could die in that short stretch, how many more had been claimed in the fifteen miles of rails along that river? How many are similarly trapped in the countless miles of rails that crisscross the nation? Here is a creature with few, if any, natural enemies and a life span of up to 138 years. Yet, seeking only warmth, it finds technology and death.

As I stood hip-deep in the river and cast tiny flies to an occasional rising trout, I remained unsettled by what I had seen. Yet it was not the plight of the box turtles that bothered me most. I knew I had no answers for them, nor would I seek any. That is precisely the problem. Virtually everywhere we look, we are confronted with environmental problems both large and small for which there seem to be no easy solutions. Perhaps no solutions at all. Indeed, many of the problems are so knotted and confused that it seems hopeless to even seek an answer.

Those box turtles were trapped by more than just rails; they were caught in the kind of deadly trade-off that is becoming more and more common. Sure, a railroad bed could be designed to prevent their entrapment, but it would never be constructed. It would be too expensive, there are too many miles of track, and box turtles are understandably a low priority for the rail industry. Furthermore, no studies have been made to determine the extent of the problem. Which means that a certain unknown number of box turtles have been, and will continue to be, expendable — sacrificed to the greater benefits we all share from railroads. And if there is blame to be placed, is it not therefore shared by us all?

More wildlife is killed on our highways each year than by all other means combined. The automobile is wildlife's biggest predator, yet except for the erection of a few Deer Crossing and Chipmunk Crossing signs, what has ever been done? What can be done? For every environmental battle we fight and win, we lose countless others, and in many cases we don't even choose to fight. Instead, we simply accept the loss as a necessary and unavoidable price for progress. And ironically, some of our energy is wasted in bitter contests that should never even occur. For example, many well-meaning people seek to ban hunting, yet regulated hunting has no adverse effect on wildlife. In fact, the money spent on management and habitat improvement from licenses and taxes on sporting gear protects and enhances wildlife populations. Without it, many species — and not just those sought by sportsmen — would be far less numerous than they are today. Meanwhile, our heritage of wildlife and natural resources is slipping away.

A few box turtles trapped on a railroad may indeed be expendable, but we face other sacrifices that are far more critical. Countless pesticides are being pumped into the environment, virtually without regard to their impact on wildlife. Again, far too little is known about their effects, not just on wildlife, but on human life as well. The long-term impact could be as disastrous to the earth's life as all-out nuclear war, yet most of us seem no more concerned about it than we are about a few sun-baked box turtles. Solutions may exist, but we don't seek them effectively. It can't be helped, we say. Agriculture is essential, and some loss is inevitable. But at what point does the loss balance the gain? Will we even recognize that point, and can we afford to wait that long?

The same is true of our rapidly disappearing woodlands, wetlands, and other undeveloped wild areas. Taken individually, the loss of habitat to a shopping center, a cloverleaf, or a housing development may not seem drastic, but the overall trend is frightening. Someday, if we last that long, we may be in the Supreme Court fighting to save the last half-acre vacant lot in the middle of a megalopolis extending from Key West to Nova Scotia.

When I left the river that day, I walked along the tracks to the car. A box turtle (the one I had saved?) was at the edge of the gravel, climbing toward the rails. I carried him to the car and put him in a small cardboard box. One turtle, heading to Raleigh, a shell within a shell moving at 55 miles per hour, his future beyond his control. I felt an intense kinship.

A Brief History of Hats

There were several dozen straw hats hanging on the wall in the feed store, but one was different. It had a front brim of green plastic, a feature I hadn't seen in years. I paid the man $6.95 for it, stuck it on my head, and headed for the truck with a sack of fertilizer on my shoulder. I was barely out the door before I was whistling a straw hat song:

Blue skies
Smiling at me,
Nothing but blue skies
Do I see . . .

All I needed was a cane pole and a can of worms. I knew where to find them.

For those who might not recall, a green-brimmed straw hat was the definitive unisex garden and angling chapeau of the 1940s and 1950s, worn by everyone from grand-maws and great-"aints" to field hands and gentlemen farmers. It instantly called to mind my ample grand-mother picking beans or pulling corn in the hot sun or my grandfather sitting in a juniper boat under the cypress on Williams' Pond. They'd have been wearing such a hat. And so, for that matter, would every fair, freckled maiden who ever posed for a calendar portrait with a wheat stem in her teeth.

Like most men with thinning thatch, I'm a sucker for a hat, but only hats that can go fishing or hunting. Truth is, I never wear a hat at any other time, although I have accumulated such an astonishing number and variety that I am obliged to consider myself an expert on the subject. In my opinion, a straw hat is still the nearly ideal casual fishing hat, but it's for contemplative fishermen of another era. Unless you tie it around your neck with 1,500-pound test parachute cord, you can't keep it on at 70 miles per hour in a modern bass boat. Indeed, the changing nature of fishing has forced the retirement of other formerly practical fishing hats.

One of my earliest memories is of my dad fly fishing for black bass on the Little Alligator and Chowan Rivers while wearing a brown, canvas-covered pith helmet. It was light-weight and provided both shade and cooling circulation. But more important, whenever Dad happened to flub a backcast in a brisk crosswind, the bass bug would simply bounce off the back of his helmet like a walnut falling on a tin roof.

Aside from the double-duty straw hat, people of my grandfather's generation seldom bought a hat purely for fishing. Instead, a dapper Sunday-go-to-meeting felt fe-dora would become a fishing hat whenever Grandma said it was becoming too disreputable to wear anywhere else. I still have one of my grandfather's battered felt hats. He wore it because it kept the yellowflies from biting his bald head. You may have noticed that yellowflies (deerflies) like to land on your head, and you can beat yourself silly trying to swat them. However, an old felt hat that has been soaked in 6-12 insect repellent and flue-cured in the smoke of countless five-cent Muriel Senators will discour-age even the most determined yellowfly.

About ten years ago, while in an adventurous spirit, I bought one of those expensive raw wool Irish fishing hats that were briefly in vogue. Although it was heavy and hot, I thought it gave me a certain *je ne sais quoi.* Turned out, I was right.

"You need to lose that miserable lid," a friend finally

told me. "You look like a bad poet." That was too close to the truth, so I took his advice.

Out West, you see a lot of fishermen wearing high-dollar beaver-felt Stetsons or those straw cowboy hats called "goat ropers." I thought I might cut a dashing figure fishing in a cowboy hat, but decided not to buy one after calculating the odds that I would be confused with Gabby Hayes or some vacationing Californian (a risky association in cow country). Besides, cowboy hats tend to blow off and float away unless you staple them to your head.

If you're not into high fashion, political statements, or dude ranch role-playing, you've probably been wearing a cheap advertising freebie — one of those generic baseball caps. They shade your eyes, and you can't beat the price. On the debit side, they won't shed a light drizzle, and even a good one will last only a few months. Besides, they don't offer your ears any protection from direct sun or indirect hooks.

In recent years — and against my better instincts — I have more or less settled on one of those Florida-style Daffy Duck bonefish caps with the long bills and fold-down rear flaps. They are reasonably aerodynamic and lightweight, they shade your eyes nicely, and they protect your ears and neck from the sun. Those made of Gore-Tex will shed rain. Alas, they look ridiculous enough to provoke snickers even from other fishermen. And if you don't want a white one, you'll have to settle for purple, turquoise, or some equally obnoxious color.

Actually, when it comes to fishing hats, I think I may have come full circle. My new straw with its green brim is virtually identical to the first fishing hat I ever owned. I thought that hat was perfect when I was eight years old, and it may still be.

Besides, I can't paddle 70 miles per hour anyway.

Ship of Frogs

The old cigar box had not been opened since I was a child, yet when I saw it in the attic, I knew it held magic. Inside I found some of the things that had been important to me so many years ago: a beanshooter (you might call it a slingshot), a powerful magnifying glass, a dried turtle shell, a small rubber-band-powered speargun, a deck of playing cards with fish species on the back, a tube of BBs, a broken pocketknife, fishhooks, a tiny but functional bow and arrow, and a raccoon's foot.

There were also marbles, an old coin or two, a Cracker-Jacks prize, and a number of other items, but these were of lesser interest to me then — and now. The most prized possessions were those toys that had introduced me to the adventure and mystery of the natural world.

Like most kids, I was both protector and terrorist. I bought turtles at the dime store, peeled the pink paint from their shells, and nurtured them to health, yet I spent hours trying to develop that rubber-band speargun into an effective weapon for the huge bullfrogs that lived in the ditch in front of the house.

I used the magnifying glass to study countless bugs, marvel at the colored scales in a butterfly wing, or watch ants milk aphids. But I confess I also sizzled a few ants by directing the sun's rays on them. An injured bird was a special project requiring Popsicle-stick splints and eye-dropper feedings, yet I would hunt sparrows with an air rifle until I ran out of BBs.

The typical kid mixes stewardship and harvest, a blend that I suspect is entirely natural. I think of a friend of mine, a noted entomologist, who confided that his life-long fascination with insects began when he fed ants to ant lions in the sandy soil under a shed in his backyard. His special interest now is rare beetles.

"I was absolutely charmed by the life around me, by the variety and the violence," he says now. "What was merely an interest has grown into a career, and feeding ants to ant lions may well have been the impetus for it. I can tell you this, I learned early that sentiment does not exist in the natural world I studied. But most of all, I developed a lasting curiosity about things, and it is just as intense today as it was when I was twelve years old. And I think I've given back more than I ever took."

I can't trace my own interest and career in the outdoors to any specific thing, but I was fortunate enough to have parents and grandparents who encouraged it. Some adults seem to know exactly how to focus youthful curiosity and introduce kids to the adventure and mystery around them. David Williams's grandfather certainly did.

"My brother Skip and I had been trying to catch some bullfrogs in this pond, and our grandfather came up with an incredible scheme," said David. "He told us to get a wide plank and tie a long string to one end of it, then mount a candle upright in the middle of the plank.

"When it gets dark, he told us, you light the candle and slowly pull the plank along the edge of the pond. The candle will attract all sorts of moths and other insects, and the bullfrogs will leap up on the plank and sit there catching the insects. We thought it was a swell idea, and we set it all up just the way he told us.

"That evening, we lit the candle and skirted the edge of the pond with a string until we got back to the pier, then we waited until we figured enough insects had been attracted. We could hear those old bullfrogs jug-a-rumming around that pond, and we began to pull the plank along the edge. I'll never forget how excited we were. We were absolutely convinced that when that plank rounded the last bunch of cattails, it would be stacked up with bullfrogs.

"You know something? There wasn't a danged frog on that board, but I guess it was a good thing, because we had never stopped to figure out how we were going to get all those frogs off the plank and into our sack. It was a heck of an idea, though."

Who knows whether that caper had anything to do with David's career as wildlife artist and illustrator, but it was surely a significant chapter in his introduction to the great outdoors. It wouldn't surprise me to learn that every naturalist, every outdoorsman, could tell similar tales. And somewhere among their childhood toys may be a box of memories filled with such things as turtle shells and beanshooters. Nor would it surprise David to learn that in his attic back home are a plank, a candle, and some string — a ship of frogs whose real cargo was a lifelong love of nature's mysteries.

Brothers of the Lodge

If you've ever wondered what happens to old *National Geographics*, *Reader's Digests*, and sporting magazines, you need look no farther than a hunting or fishing lodge. A lodge or camp is the final resting place of every old magazine after it passes through a prolonged purgatory in some dentist's office, a lengthy limbo in a barbershop, and forty-odd years in an attic.

Most of us have spent some marvelously happy times in such camps, and it's amazing how similar they all are. Dark, knotty pine or varnished log walls are covered with old calendars of bird dogs on points or blondes selling auto parts. There are shirttails from missed deer, cute signs ("The worst day fishing is better than the best day working"), moldy mounted fish, moth-eaten whitetails, at least one "jackalope," and the worst collection of outdoor art this side of kindergarten.

There are a poker table, an assortment of greasy, overstuffed chairs, a side table covered with the aforementioned magazines, and half the parts to a game of Parcheesi. Lampshades are festooned with old popping bugs and trout flies. Decoys and fishing tackle are scattered everywhere, and there might be an ancient outboard or a stack of deer stands leaning in a corner beside the gun cabinet. The interior is lit no better than a neighborhood bar, which is appropriate because there will also be a bar covered with half-empty bottles. (The truly dead soldiers will be under the front porch.)

The less said about the kitchen, the better, but the most lasting impression is likely to be how diligent the rats have been in leaving their calling cards in every dish and coffee cup.

The smell of a fishing or hunting camp is a combination of cigar and wood smoke, old canvas, insect repellent, wet wool, wet dogs, and fried eggs (the only foolproof hot food), overlaid with the faint, binding aroma of Hoppes No. 9 powder solvent. (Note to women: Have you considered wearing Hoppes as a perfume? It would be highly effective.)

Those of us who hunt and fish obsessively — that's redundant, isn't it? — figure that heaven must be sort of like a big hunting lodge. It's a comfortable spot after a long day, or a long life. We can pile sodden clothes in front of a fire or cast-iron stove, snooze on a collapsing sofa under a favorite book, and occasionally reach the glass on the floor. That kind of evening, after a day of fishing or hunting, sets the world back on its feet.

But it's not always quiet. I recall some years ago staying at a lodge on Currituck Sound with a bunch of elderly and friendly West Virginians. It was a good group, but somewhat given to celebration after a day afield. In the three days we were there, they must have gone through two tons of cracked ice. Numerous times each night, beginning after supper and lasting more or less indefinitely, they would suddenly lurch together at some undetectable cue (undetectable to us, at least) and raucously sing this song:

> Every time I go to town,
> The boys all kick my dog around.
> Makes no difference if he's a hound,
> You oughta not kick my dog around.

Upon completion of this warning about the evils of city living, they would resume normal conversation as though nothing at all had happened. In the wee hours of the night, we might be treated to yet another chorus delivered from their various bedrooms, where they had apparently awakened and launched into song, again on mysterious cue. It is apparently the kind of thing that develops among long, close friends, and we were not very much put out. Indeed, I came to like them and their song.

It was this same group that bequeathed my companion and me what may have been the finest — and certainly the fullest — meal either of us ever ate. The wife of the lodge owner appeared at the dinner table one evening bearing a huge platter of softshell crabs. I have seen smaller piles of discarded tires. The proprietress left, but as we prepared to feast we noted that the West Virginians seemed riveted in shock.

"What in hell's them?" one said finally.

"Softshell crabs," said my delighted companion.

Simultaneously, they all pushed back their chairs, arose, and headed for the door.

"You don't want any?" we asked incredulously.

"We ain't eating no spiders," came the reply.

We ate the spiders. We ate all the spiders while from the next room, accompanied by the tinkling of ice in glasses, our insect-fearing companions burst into song.

There may come a time when there are no more hunting and fishing lodges or camps. There may be no wild places left, no wilderness to nurture the creatures that bring folks like us together. No spiders, no hounds to love and kick around, no sparkling streams or placid lakes, no big woods or lespedeza fields, no choral camaraderie. But I hope I'm wrong, and in any event, I suspect by that time I'll be long gone to that great lodge in the sky, where there will surely be a few old magazines around for the memories.

Fly Fishing for Grouse

I quote herewith a report by Charlie Carson that appeared in the Fall 1985 issue of the *Flyline*, a newsletter published by the North Carolina Council of Trout Unlimited:

> Bud Hunter from Hendersonville was fly fishing on the Tuckasegee River in Jackson County recently and brought along his old bird dog, Pal. As Bud was fishing, Pal was in the laurel thickets in search of grouse. One flushed and flew directly over Bud as he was making a backcast. The bird became tangled in the leader and took ten yards of line; however, the 6x tippet broke and the grouse took his favorite fly and continued flying downstream. Although I was on the trip fishing elsewhere, Alex Bernhardt from Lenoir was with Bud and swears that this tale is true.

This report has the ring of truth and, moreover, has the potential for revolutionizing the sport of grouse hunting. It has long been recognized that one of the disadvantages of hunting is the inability to come up with any sort of catch-and-release mechanism that could prove workable. Discounting those hunters who have solved this problem by simply missing all their shots, there has heretofore been no way to collect a bag limit and also release it no worse for wear. Or, to put it in the jargon of professional wildlife enforcement officers, once a critter has been "reduced to possession," there is no way to "enlarge it to freedom."

But suppose you could combine the best elements of

fishing with those of hunting and come up with a workable combination? It appears that that's what Bud and Pal
have done. There remain, however, some unanswered
questions. If a 6x leader is too light, then what test leader
would hold an adult grouse? Obviously, 1x would be unsporting, but what about 4x or 5x? Would bamboo fly
rods be suitable, or should the grouse angler choose a
graphite or boron rod? It would seem that a glass rod
might be a violation of propriety, and certainly no sporting grouse angler would stoop to a casting or spinning
rod.

Furthermore, our reporter is typically obscure in naming the fly pattern that proved successful in this instance,
saying only that the grouse took Bud's "favorite fly." 'Fess
up, fellows, was it a grouse and teal pattern, a soft-hackled
partridge, or something else? I'm only guessing, but I'll
bet it was a terrestrial, since it is a fact that grouse like
beetles, ants, and other insects as well as fruit and berries.

This brings up another point. Would grouse anglers be
restricted to the use of artificial imitations, or might there
be certain covers set aside where it was permissible to use
natural bait? If so, I foresee a controversy, because it is all
too clear that mortality will be higher for grouse that gulp
a succulent fox grape threaded on a Mustad than for
grouse lightly hooked in the beak by a carefully wrought
imitation grape made of hair from a purple deer. Would
grouse anglers claim that a bird on a hand-tied fly is worth
two on a bush bait? Would it be considered unsporting to
hook a grouse on the ground? — must one cast only to
rising birds? Would there be a great hue and cry to pro-
mote the stocking of fingerling grouse in areas where
populations ebbed? These are not mere questions of
proper regulation and management; they seek the higher
ground of ethical behavior.

I can't settle these matters here, but this whole business

reminds me of an incident I witnessed some years ago when I dropped in to visit a friend one afternoon. He was out in the woodlot behind the house stalking those little striped lizards called skinks. He wanted to photograph them, but they were not in the mood. They were also a good bit quicker than he was, but alas, not quite as clever. Using a ten-foot surf rod, he had run monofilament through the guides so that a small loop protruded from the tip. Although the skinks would not let him approach any closer than about eight feet, they were not alarmed by the rod, and he was able to creep within reaching distance and slip the almost invisible loop over their heads. Then, by pulling on the monofilament, he could close the loop around their necks and reduce them to possession.

He was so fascinated by this advance in technology and the sporting qualities of the capture that he had totally forgotten why he had ever wanted to catch them in the first place. When I arrived, he had already captured half a dozen and gently released them, and he was now concentrating on only the most wary skinks.

"I think I'm onto something here," he whispered excitedly, so as not to alarm his prey. "With the proper exposure, this could become a national sport. Chapters of Skinks Unlimited would be formed, and members would hold annual fund-raising banquets and auction paintings of skinks. I've already determined that a proper skink rod would be about twelve feet long and have a very delicate tip action. Graphite, because of its light weight, would be ideal. Skillful skinkers could play them on cobwebby 8X leaders."

I must have looked a bit dubious, because he paused a moment, apparently lost in thought. "Of course, they don't jump much," he added as he unjointed his surf rod and leaned it against the woodshed.

We walked back to the house and sat on the porch. "You don't think the world is ready for this, do you?" he asked. "Well," I answered, choosing my words carefully, "most of the world's great thinkers have been ahead of their time."

Too Lazy to Fish

Fishing, especially fishing for pleasure, has long been considered a trifling pursuit. It is no coincidence that the word "fisherman" follows the phrase "good for nothing" almost as frequently as eggs follow ham.

The late Reverend George Washington Bethune was well acquainted with angling's dubious reputation. In the mid-1800s, he was one of this nation's most prominent clergymen and a noted writer and publisher. He was also an avid angler—an affliction he took no small pains to hide.

In Bethune's era, fishing was considered even more trifling than it is today, and he hid his tackle en route to and from his favorite fishing holes so that his congregation would not suspect his true purpose. Furthermore, when he penned the scholarly preface to the first American edition of Izaak Walton's *The Compleat Angler* in 1847, Bethune signed it only as "The American Editor." Never mind that the relationship between fishing and preaching has a long, honorable history going back at least to Saint Peter. Bethune was taking no chances that his flock would learn of his secret passion. (One is tempted to add that his was a level of discretion much to be admired in light of modern evangelical disclosures.)

If Bethune's followers believed fishing was a waste of time, imagine what they might have thought about someone who simply sat and watched someone else fish. "Too lazy to fish" may well be the ultimate insult, yet I have known many people who, as they grew older, preferred to watch others fish. It isn't always a matter of laziness, either.

I think back nearly forty years to afternoons on an old millpond in Halifax County. I can still visualize my grandfather sitting in the rear of the boat puffing on a cigar and spilling the ashes on his coat and tie. Grandpa would make a few casts from time to time, but he spent far more time paddling and watching me fish. If we approached a particularly good spot to catch a largemouth bass, he'd point it out to me.

"A good one hangs around that old stump," he'd say. "I'll hold the boat here while you try for him."

"But you always give me the good spots," I'd protest weakly.

"I'd rather see you catch him," he'd say.

If I felt a bit guilty, it was only because we both knew that I would rather see me catch him, too. That's hardly unusual at the age of ten, when I was too young to understand my grandfather's motives, or my father's. Dad routinely made similar sacrifices for my brothers and me, giving us the best seats in the duck blind, or making certain we had the best and safest shooting angles on the covey rise when Buck's nose was full of Eau d'Bobwhite.

At the time, it seemed to be an act of immense unselfishness, but I know better now. Indeed, it may be as much fun to pass along an obsession as it ever was to acquire it.

Watching a child catch a fish is one of life's great pleasures, and there is scant difference between that first tiny bluegill caught with the help of a grandfather, and the one you help your grandchild catch.

Some years ago, I watched as my daughter, Susan, successfully stalked and landed her first big cutthroat on a tiny fly in Idaho. A few days later, she landed a big rainbow on a Madison River float in Montana. Would it have pleased me as much to catch those fish myself? Not quite. Likewise, I was on hand when my son, Scott, landed his first Spanish mackerel on the end of an Outer Banks pier, and again when he caught his first big bass on a topwater plug in Lake Mattamuskeet. Would I have swapped places with him? Well, I suppose in all honesty it would depend upon just how big that bass happened to be.

There have been many such "sharings," and I hope there will be more. And if fishing or watching others fish is trifling, then I have not only wasted a significant part of my life but have also helped a passel of blood relatives and good friends waste theirs. I'm no less guilty — and certainly no more repentant — than the late Reverend Bethune.

A Few Kind Words about Guns

"Return with me to those thrill-packed days of yesteryear." The voice belongs to Bruce Dunbar, radio announcer for Merita Bread. It is 6:30 P.M. any Monday, Wednesday, or Friday in the late 1940s and early 1950s. Suppertime. Lone Ranger time.

"From out of the past comes the thunder of hoofbeats and a hearty Hi-Yo, Silver," Dunbar says, his voice rising as the *William Tell* Overture fills the kitchen. Mom and Dad sit silently eating, exchanging an occasional bemused glance. I'm so carried away that I've accidentally eaten a butterbean.

Rossini's stirring music climaxes in a burst of shots, and Brace Beamer — the real Lone Ranger — urges the big horse Silver faster and faster until we are all galloping together through the long summer twilight. (Who is this Clayton Moore impostor, anyway?)

It was a time when my friends and I — barefoot, tanned, streaked with sweaty dirt — ran the alleys and backyards every summer day armed to the teeth. Some of us were cowboys. Others were Indians, by choice. We swapped off. When we couldn't be the Lone Ranger or Crazy Horse, we'd settle for the Durango Kid, or any other wrangler who didn't sing or cheat on his horse by kissing some girl.

The only problem with pretending you were the Lone Ranger's faithful Indian sidekick was that Tonto usually went into town to get supplies and got the snot beat out of him by some local toughs. And the Lone Ranger, who was camped in a cottonwood grove on the north side of town (always the north side), would rescue him in a hail of

silver bullets. Of course, Tonto did the rescuing sometimes, but we weren't yet mature enough to appreciate his
gentle nature. Now, Crazy Horse and Red Cloud were
another matter. They didn't take no guff.

When I was about eight or nine years old, my cap pistols
got some serious competition from my first real gun — a
Daisy Red Ryder lever-action carbine with a wood stock
and a rawhide thong hanging from a ring alongside the
action. With it came tubes of BBs and an exhaustive introduction to safety and ethics from Dad, Mom, Grandpa,
and every other relative who could gain an audience.

"Treat every gun as though it is loaded, and never
point it at anyone even for the briefest moment," my father told me. Two motivations enforced those conditional
instructions. I was being truly trusted for perhaps the first
time in my life, and that meant a lot. I also knew I might
lose the gun if I got caught misusing it.

For a lot of kids growing up in the rural South in those
days, the gift of a BB gun was the first real test of responsibility. It was a darn good one, but only when that gift
came with proper instruction. For those so entrusted, safe
gun use became a matter of honor, something we were
proud to know, proud to demonstrate.

As for me, I spent some of the happiest days of my life in
dusty fields and along dirt roads in Northampton County,
pockets bulging with tubes of BBs and the carbine always
in hand. I was a mountain man disjuncted by birth to the
flat pine East, walking the plowed rows, skirting the mysterious swamps. My provisions were raw peanuts straight
from the stack, and a sweet stalk of sugarcane.

I filed the sights to correct my Daisy's tendency to shoot
slightly to the left, and I could pick off a Tru-Ade bottle
cap at twenty feet riding past at a dead gallop on my stick
pinto. Dry dirt clods in plowed fields were favorite targets,
because a hit yielded a satisfying puff of dust, proof of

developing marksmanship, not unlike the ricocheting shots of a favorite Saturday matinee hero. Tin cans pinged nicely, but I was warned not to shoot bottles. Too many barefoot cowboys in these parts.

A confession: One day I impulsively gunned down one of my grandmother's beloved catbirds in the hedge beside the smokehouse. That transgression cost me a sore rump and the temporary loss of my carbine. But I learned the difference between shooting mere tin cans and hunting. In addition to safety, a proper hunter must have an intricate code of ethics, respect for the quarry, and a tradition of ensuring that hunted populations prosper. Being an honorary Indian, I could understand that.

A few years later, when the air piston on my carbine finally played out after about a million shots, Santa left a .22 rifle under the tree with my name on it. I never thought of it as a symbol of war or crime, as so many do today, but rather as proof of my parents' confidence in me.

I hope the era isn't ending when a kid can walk out his back door with a Red Ryder and find a field full of dirt clods, a woodlot full of wonder, and the ghosts of long-dead cowboys and Indians. Not to mention a sense of responsibility.

But I'm not sure. Looks to me as though the cottonwood grove on the north side of town is being clear-cut, paved, and malled.

Camp Cooking Catastrophes

Back when I used to do a lot of camping and out-door cooking (note use of the past tense), I was a sucker for a crisp fall day. I could picture myself camped along some river where the smoke from my cookfire curled against the misty mountains and the air was laden with the rich aroma of perking coffee and sizzling bacon. I went to a lot of trouble to bring that mental picture to reality, but after years of failure, I have decided that the whole image of carefree campfire cooking is a myth.

Certainly the Boy Scouts unwittingly played a part in this deception. At the age of ten — before there were such things as centerfolds — I would spend hours studying the Boy Scout manual, captivated by step-by-step illustrations showing how to make a proper cookfire, prepare pemmi-can, or construct various utensils out of green sticks and vines. I recall trying to make a reflector oven out of tin cans, which (the plans said) could be quickly snipped and folded into shape. I got off easy on that one — only seven stitches.

Then there was the time I saw an illustration in *Boy's Life* showing how to make bannock by twisting dough around a stick and baking it over a fire. I'm not sure what I expected, but the resulting spiral of bread had the shape and resilience of a rhododendron walking stick. I suppose you could have nibbled on it while you hiked, but you'd have needed the dental work of a beaver.

I was especially vulnerable to the image of a coffeepot and kettle hanging over the fire, on a branch supported by two forked sticks. Even before I'd pitch my tent on a camping trip, I'd grab my trusty hatchet and head for the nearest woods to seek out forked sticks. You'd be surprised how much variance there is between forked sticks. During my Scout years, I probably defoliated more forests than Agent Orange looking for a perfectly matched pair.

Of course, I knew campers who carried a sleeping bag full of candy bars, square Nabs, and cans of pork'n'beans to tide them over between meals, but that was cheating. Those of us following in the footsteps of Daniel Boone and Jeremiah Johnson wanted hot meals. Let the sissies hide in their tents and eat candy bars; I wanted a real meal cooked over a fire — hot dogs charred beyond recognition or marshmallows that burned with a handsome blue flame.

Actually, I recall one culinary triumph during those early years. My mother took a tin coffee can, washed it thoroughly, and filled it with layers of onions, hamburger, and sliced potatoes. She added salt, pepper, and a bit of water, then put the tin top on it. "Put this in the fire for thirty minutes, and when you take the top off it's ready to eat," she told me. "It's called a coffee can casserole."

For once I enjoyed a fine meal, despite the ashes that fell into the can when I pried open the lid and the third-degree burns on both hands.

Similar disasters plagued me through Scouthood into adulthood. There was the time a plastic spoon melted in a pot of tomato soup, a mishap that was discovered only after enough soup had been eaten to reveal the unmelted tip of the handle in the bottom of the pot. Or the time we poured a dozen eggs into a red-hot skillet and were astounded to see a giant yellow bubble form instantly. It burst just as we dove for cover.

You don't see stuff like that written up in camp cooking literature. They don't warn you about exploding eggs or melting spoons. Nor do they ever show anyone trying to cook in a monsoon while huddled around a smoking hunk of soggy pine under a quivering tent fly that is rapidly filling with several hundred gallons of water.

I know you're nodding your head and thinking, "He knows, he knows." And you're right—I do know. I think I've experienced most of the calamities that afflict those who cook outdoors, not to mention the aftermath that befalls those who eat the results.

Anyway, I was reminded of all this when I received a promotional leaflet from a tent manufacturer. The literature extolled the joys of camping, and the piece on camp cooking began with this statement: "Camp cooking can be a vacation from kitchen chores with the right preparation . . ."

Who do those folks think they're kidding? Bet that writer never ate a fried sardine.

Blindfolded, with Scissors

This is a story about a crab, sort of. We were at the beach and decided that we wanted some blue crabs steamed Maryland-style. We went to the sound, where it was simple enough to attract the crabs by tying weighted fish heads to string and tossing the bait into the water along the edges of deeper cuts or around piers. When a crab would grab the fish head, we'd pull it within range of our long-handled nets.

Back at the cottage, we iced down the crabs to keep them alive and make them inactive. We put several inches of vinegar — we could have used beer — in the bottom of a large pot and dropped in a rack to keep the crabs out of the liquid. Then we began filling the pot with layers of live crabs, sprinkling each layer liberally with flake salt and Old Bay seasoning. Old Bay works fine if you can't get one of the special seasonings from a Baltimore or Eastern Shore crab house.

We kept adding layers of live crabs and seasoning until the pot was filled, then put the lid on so we could steam them quickly. Or tried to. The pot was too full. We re-arranged the top layers of crabs several times, but soon it became clear that we had exactly one crab too many.

"Oh well, then, take one out," someone said with exasperation. I gingerly grasped a crab by the back flipper, avoiding its claws. There seemed to be only one thing to do with it. I carried it out the door and down to the beach. There I washed off the salt and seasoning, then watched as one blue crab, lucky beyond knowing, scuttled out to sea.

I think of that crab from time to time. He — it was a male — seems to represent the random, often whimsical, and utterly capricious nature of life. Who stays in the pot? Who gets a reprieve? And, like the crab, how often do we survive a close shave without even knowing it? Daily? More often?

I'm not sure that hunters or fishermen face threats more frequently than anyone else, but ours are more inventive. Not long after the incident with the crab, I was fishing with a friend in a borrowed boat near Harker's Island. It was one of those handsome, lapstrake, wooden Barbour outboards that were so popular during the late 1950s and early 1960s. This one had seen better days, however, and we were not surprised that the boat seemed to be leaking. No cause for alarm, we figured, because we could bail it out if it got too deep. We continued fishing. As usual, I was puffing on my pipe, and my companion was smoking cigarettes.

By midafternoon, we began to smell gas — not much at first, and besides, all motorboats smell like gas. We kept fishing until the floorboards were awash. When my companion began to rummage around in the bilges looking for something to use as a bailer, he made a hair-raising discovery. A seam had split in the eighteen-gallon tank. We had been wading ankle-deep in gasoline for at least an hour. Since we were both smoking, we were little more than a pair of Molotov cocktails with short fuses.

To this day, I don't know why our crisp body parts weren't found all over Cape Lookout, but somehow we got our smokes extinguished, patched the tank, and bailed most of the gasoline. Even as we were being towed in, my companion was prepared to ride his lucky streak: He jokingly wondered whether it might be possible for him to let himself out behind the boat on a tethered cushion so he could safely light up.

On another occasion, I left a well-marked mountain trail to take a rugged shortcut down to the trout stream I planned to fish. While on my hands and knees trying to extract my fly rod from some especially thick rhododendron, I put my foot out to stand up and found that it was hanging over the edge of a well-hidden four-hundred-foot precipice. Had I not snagged my line on the rhododendron, I believe I would have walked right out into midair just like Wile E. Coyote.

In both those instances, I became aware of the danger, but maybe it's best that we don't know how often we are spared — that we aren't aware the driver we just passed has a snootful and is going to hit the very next car head-on.

Small wonder that we grow cautious as we grow older. We may have less to lose with each passing day, but we are increasingly loathe to lose it. We have seen too many mindless crabs scuttle to sea. We drive slowly and keep both hands on the wheel. We look before we leap, then often don't leap. We count no chickens before they hatch; indeed, we are unwilling to acknowledge that any have ever hatched.

Be kind if you see someone wading a trout stream with unnecessary care or wearing enough blaze orange to be visible from a satellite. It might be me, or someone else who's learned that we run through life blindfolded, carrying sharp scissors.

Breaking In a New Guide

In the early morning, the cool night air would descend from the mountains around us, bringing with it the scent of fir trees. The aroma would linger—like Christmas in July—until the rising sun heated the sage-pocked Montana river valley along the upper Madison River and pushed the heady aroma back up the slopes. It seemed an especially appropriate salutation for each of the ten days in 1986 we stayed in the cluster of lodgepole pine cabins called the Slide Inn.

From the porch of our cabin, we could look across the river to the wide gap in the mountains known as Raynold's Pass. Jim Bridger's men had camped there, and Indians long before him. From the looks of things, it could have been yesterday. The inn was very comfortably rustic and took its name from Slide Lake just upstream, which was formed in 1959 when an earthquake caused an entire mountaintop to slide into the river.

Susan and Scott loved the Slide Inn, partly because its name sounded so wonderfully low and sleazy and thus had predictable appeal for youth. (Susan was just seventeen; Scott was twenty-one.) From this base camp, their father was ostensibly introducing them to the glories of the American West. More precisely, he was making a return pilgrimage to fly fish his favorite trout streams in Montana, Wyoming, and Idaho with two eager gillies.

The fishing was varied and often good. We waded the Madison and tried our luck on streams in Yellowstone National Park. On several days, we made junkets to fish for rainbows on the Henry's Fork of the Snake River in

Idaho. By midweek, Scott had taken a dandy brown on a big nymph on a float down the Ashton to Chester stretch of the lower Henry's Fork, and Susan had fooled some nice cutthroats on tiny caddis in a headwater. Their already keen fly-fishing skills were being honed daily, but it was Susan who was to display them most memorably.

We had learned that the salmon flies—actually large stone flies—were beginning to hatch as expected on the Madison, and on the day before we were to fly home, we waited at the Slide Inn for our guide to arrive. He pulled up driving a new red Audi and hauling the most expensive drift boat money could buy. Everything he owned was high-dollar new, and he had an attitude to match.

"I wasn't told I would be carrying kids," he said, looking at Susan and Scott, though he couldn't have been more than about twenty-five himself. "I don't know about this, but if you can keep from hooking me on a backcast, we'll try it."

As we loaded our gear and launched the boat, he swaggered around sharing his superior knowledge of fishing and making disparaging remarks about our tackle. Susan shot me a sidelong glance. I could tell you the word that formed on her lips, but I think it best not to.

Our guide motioned me to get up front and fish. I shook my head and handed Susan the 8½-foot, 7-weight rod already equipped with a big stone-fly nymph and strike indicator. Mister Personality would surely have paid dearly for a suit of armor, but he said nothing.

Susan jammed her legs in the supports at the bow, and the boat swung into the current, with the guide at the oars. As we bounced down the swift current and slid past huge boulders steaming in whitewater, the guide began to shout orders. Susan ignored him as she faced the bank, made a couple of deft double-hauls, and shot seventy feet of line to a glassy boil next to the bank. As the current swept the line downstream, she expertly threw a long mend upstream. Lefty Kreh couldn't have done it better.

The guide looked as though he'd been gut-shot. I glanced at Scott, who wore a curious smile and seemed to be intently studying the clouds.

"Ah, don't worry, you'll get the hang of it," I said to Susan.

"Yeah, gotta watch those tailing loops beyond about eighty feet," she answered as she made another superb cast, adding a sophisticated midcast mend.

The advice from the rowing seat fell off sharply as we swept down the river. Moments later, the strike indicator dipped and Susan set the hook into a big rainbow. By the time our guide had slipped the net under that fish, he'd fallen in love. It was a miraculous transformation. The swagger was gone and the advice was tempered. We were four anglers on equal footing, sharing a rare moment of privilege on a wonderful river.

Susan caught the biggest rainbows, and the most, but Scott and I did well enough. We left the guide a nice tip — he'd earned it — and a promise to fish together again. It had been a grand day, and valuable lessons were learned all around. Even so, when we flew home the following day, only one "kid" had the guts to wear his Slide Inn T-shirt. Care to guess who that was?

Life on the End

It takes several days to get into it: to stop making notes of things suddenly remembered, errands forgotten, duties undone, responsibilities shirked. Out there, a thousand feet from the beach, the pilings shift with the green swells, and one hears only the occasional hiss of water and the distant laughter of children. That and the sounds made by fishermen who are unhurried and not always terribly hopeful.

"Be some blues in with the tide," says one as he flips a cigarette over the rail. "Outside the sandbar. Maybe." He leans there, staring out to sea with no expectation that anyone might answer him.

Later someone says, "Need a little change in the weather."

"Wouldn't hurt," says his companion, reaching to tug on a set line that anchors a live bait. "Your blue is fixing to get around that other line over there unless you tighten up a little."

A family appears on the end of the pier: man, wife, and two daughters. They look bored and as pale as Michelangelo sculptures. Nothing is happening — nothing appears to have ever happened — but the question is always asked. Several hundred times a day. "Anybody getting anything?"

"Spanish last evening," someone answers. "No kings since whenever."

"Spanish?" the father repeats. It is clear that he doesn't understand the answer. But he and his family have completed the annual vacation ritual — they have walked to the end of the pier.

Actually, the fishermen barely notice. After two days on a pier, you could not say with certainty whether tomorrow is Wednesday, or possibly Thursday. After a week, you no longer care. Your body rhythms and senses have been redirected. The ears hear only the click of a reel or the flop of a fish on the hot, greasy planks. Eyes see little beyond the distant mud line, a dark patch of menhaden, or the flash of mackerel under a bait. Tuned to the tides and the wind, you are human only from 10 P.M., when you collapse in a gritty bed, until you arise at 4 A.M. and arrive on the pier shivering and holding the first of many Styrofoam cups of wretched coffee.

Some fishermen believe that fishing an ocean pier is the lowest form of angling, an overly simplistic "chunk and chance" recreation conceived to appeal to those who cannot afford a charter boat. I tend to think it is more like baseball — a subtle, perhaps even cerebral, form of angling that is an acquired taste. My perspective may be warped, but I would rather fish a pier than troll offshore. It is a question of challenge and finesse.

You see, it is a myth that pier fishing is a sport that requires no skill. Indeed, it takes many years to learn to fish a pier properly from beach wash to tip, and to do so through all the seasonal peaks. From early spring until the piers close under the lash of winter storms, there is a more or less continual change in the menu. Several dozen saltwater species can be caught from a pier from spring through fall, but ironically, their appearance is both predictable and uncertain. You may know when the bluefish, flounder, pompano, Spanish and king mackerel, puppy drum, cobia, sheepshead, spots, and sea mullet normally make their migratory entrance, but weather can advance or delay that appointment.

Not only must you know the habits and migration patterns of all these fish, you must learn dozens of different fishing techniques. Take a day in late summer or fall, for example. Beginning in the curl of the shore break, you might catch pompano and sea mullet on live softshell mole crabs. In the slough, live shrimp, minnows, or strip bait will take flounders. Spots and other bottom-feeding panfish may also be feeding in the slough on fresh shrimp or bloodworms. Farther out, just beyond the sandbar, the blues may be chasing minnows, depending upon the tide. Sheepshead will be nibbling on tiny crustaceans around the pilings. At the end of the pier, Spanish mackerel and blues will be flashing at lures, and king mackerel may be stalking a live bait.

It takes years to learn all the techniques for these and many other species, and it's a rare trip that won't reveal at least one or two new wrinkles.

It may look dull to the casual observer, but pier fishing can be as simple as you want, or as complex as you make it. And it has a certain appeal that is as timeless and hypnotic as the surf. Take your watch off when you fish a pier. You won't miss it.

Homegrown Interludes

Three pounds for a dollar. That was a deal for real tomatoes nurtured by late afternoon storms and a blazing Carteret sun. I picked only those that were ripe, since they had zero chance of surviving the weekend.

It was still early, but it was clearly going to be another scorcher, and the roadside grove was an oasis of live oaks that seemed to hold remnants of last night's ocean breeze. Just beyond the dense shade, the fields shimmered in brilliant stillness like an overexposed photograph. Insects hummed in the high grass, the hot buzz of summer.

It was pleasant there, and I was reluctant to leave the still life of squash, peppers, melons, boiled peanuts, and sweet corn. Besides, something here had tunneled into pockets of long-forgotten memory, unlocking images that had not surfaced in years. How long? — thirty years? forty? Perhaps it was the smell of vegetables that had triggered the recollection of grandmothers and aunts in sweaty cotton dresses and grimy aprons shelling butterbeans on porches and airy dogtrots. My thumbnails grew sore thinking about it. Whatever it was, I lingered and began to look around.

I inspected a jar of molasses, but it wasn't local. Probably it was as good as any, but the label was too fancy, the address too distant. The black syrup I remembered from childhood was kept in a big tin lard stand in the pantry, and because sugar was rationed during the war, my grandmother used it as a substitute. Some of it sweetened coffee and tea, but most met its destiny on the quintessential scratch biscuit, having begun its journey from a field in

Northampton County. Early each fall, we rode the mule-pulled wagon piled high with cane, sucking on the stalks until we reached the mill where that mule, or another one, walked in circles hitched to the end of a long shaft. The raw juice from the crushed cane was boiled into syrup, and every fly from Potecasi to Aulander joined us in sweet celebration.

Label notwithstanding, I bought a jar. At the end of the vegetable bins, I spotted a cooler of shrimp. I would need some bait, and unlike the shrimp I see all too often, these were fresh and firm, a translucent green with no odor. It doesn't seem to be widely appreciated that sea mullet, spots, and pompano want their shrimp absolutely fresh. It's odd, considering that fastidious humans often settle for mushy shrimp, spoiling to smelly pinkness.

A plan was gaining purchase. I would fish the piers and surf, cook my catch, and read myself into guiltless mid-morning, postlunch, and prebedtime naps. I would eat tomato sandwiches on white bread, slathered with Miracle Whip and dusted thickly with black pepper, or marinate the slices in sugar and vinegar as my grandmother had done so long ago. Maybe I would eat a tomato whole, like an apple, in honor of my grandfather. On a morning like this, he would have been in the garden at dawn, carrying a large basket, but his labor was not without pleasure, and he would graze with a puckish grin, handing me a tomato straight off the vine, cool and dewlapped. We would stand there eating, passing a saltshaker he carried back and forth. It was a strange ceremony — all the more so given that normally, at that tender age, I would not have eaten a tomato without first picking out all the seeds. But no more, and surely when this weekend was done, my face would be as pimply from the acid as a seventeen-year-old's.

One detail awaited. Invitations to the meals would have

to be extended. And, more important, the fish would have to accept them. Late that afternoon, I tried the surf for awhile unsuccessfully, then fished on the end of the pier until well past sunset. For my trouble, I had but two small Spanish mackerel. That would never be enough, unless . . . well, why not? I would eat the leftover bait. After all, the shrimp had been kept on ice, and *bait du jour* had a rather elegant ring to it.

While the small mackerel fillets were broiling in the oven, I peeled the remaining shrimp and seared them quickly on top of the stove in garlic and olive oil. The tomatoes had been in the sugar and vinegar for several hours, and the jar of molasses and a loaf of bread were waiting.

An hour later, stuffed and drowsy, I walked out onto the beach and sat in the dark facing the breakers. It had been a wonderful day, and yet, I had picked my memories too selectively and surely honored them too selfishly. How foreign my day would have seemed to those ancestors who, even in their leisure, had seldom napped or read or fished; whose laborious summer days had begun before dawn and ended at dark with peas yet to can and corn still to shuck.

I was sure of one thing, however. When their tomatoes got ripe, they'd have found time to eat them.

Out on the Big Blue

It was still very early in the morning when we headed east out of Morehead City on a nearly flat sea. We sat on the bow and marked our progress as the water shifted from pale emerald over shallow sandbars to darker shades of green at the sea buoy. Behind us, the sunwashed pastel cottages grew smaller and smaller until the sea and sky erased the faint scrim of land.

The captain did not have to tell us when we passed into the Gulf Stream. The water became an intense, deep blue with astonishing clarity. It seemed as though we were sitting on the gently curved top of some giant gemstone. Patches of yellow sargassum weed drifted past, and flying fish in twos and threes burst out ahead of the boat and sailed low over the water like skeet.

"It's a big pond out here today," said the mate, as he finished rigging the baits and snapped the lines into the outriggers. "I'm afraid we may need a little chop to get the baits to skip just right for marlin."

We trolled for several hours, catching only a bull dolphin that attacked one of the baits and was accidentally snagged in the side. Though it weighed only twenty pounds, reeling it in foul-hooked was like trying to drag in a door tethered at the knob. As the hours passed, some passengers opted for naps. I may have dozed a moment or two, but mostly I sat, legs dangling, on the back of the flying bridge, taking it all in. A trip to the Gulf Stream is too uncommon, and this was an especially handsome day to be offshore. Massive cumulus clouds billowed on the horizon, their distant reflections mirrored upside down.

Behind the gleaming white boat, the milky green turbulence of the wake contrasted sharply with the deep blue where the baits skipped.

From the bridge, the radio crackled with messages in accents that betrayed enviable Outer Banks upbringings. Some say the accent is a legacy of Elizabethan English, preserved for centuries by the isolation of these barrier islands and the nearby mainland. We listened, noting that no one seemed to be catching any more fish than we were.

"Oi've not seen it so ca'm in many years," said one captain somewhere north of us off Hatteras. "One sport up here had one on earlier, but it broke his string."

Later, in midafternoon, the wind freshened. We could see it coming miles away in dark, rippled patches, and it brought the light chop the mate wanted. Baits were re-rigged, and anglers manned the fighting chairs just in case. The water danced with the kind of energy and potential that successful anglers learn to appreciate. The baits no longer plowed like toy boats, but bounced enticingly over the chop. Another hour passed.

"Left outrigger, big fish under the bait!" shouted the mate.

From the vantage of the bridge, it looked more like a big brown log, but clearly something massive was dogging the bait.

"Marlin," confirmed the captain. "A blue about three hundred pounds, Oi'd say."

Suddenly the head broke the surface, the long bill poised ominously above the bait. "He's lit up," shouted the mate, marking the intense colors displayed by a feeding marlin. The marlin followed for a short distance, then slashed the bait violently with the bill.

"He's got it, drop back! Drop back! No, wait, he didn't take it."

With one bait down, but no marlin on it, we watched

the other as it continued to skip on the surface. "He's under that one now," said the mate quietly. "This time, immediately give him more slack, plenty of slack until I tell you to set the hook."

Again the brown log followed, and again the head emerged, lit in hues that seemed charged with electricity. As we held our breath, the huge head followed effortlessly, almost seeming detached from the bulk below. Then the bait disappeared in a foaming boil the size of a Buick.

"Drop back!" He began to count slowly. "One, two, three, four . . ."

"Is he there?" asked the angler.

The mate shook his head uncertainly. ". . . eighteen, nineteen . . ." The seconds dragged. "Now, hit him! Reel up! Hit him again!"

The line was slack. The marlin had not taken the bait. We trolled until late afternoon without raising another fish, then headed in. As we sat quietly in the dark and watched the fluorescent wake, I thought of a long-dead college professor. He had told our class that the most beautiful (his word) thing he'd ever seen was a kamikaze diving through pink, sunlit puffs of flak toward his ship. I think the professor would have liked that blue marlin.

A Train up Every Creek

When my old friend A. J. Johnson first took me trout fishing many years ago, he showed me how to catch wild browns in the Pisgah and Nantahala National Forest streams he'd been wading most of his life. But he showed me a lot more. He had accumulated a wealth of obscure history up and down many of those creeks. He knew where unremarkable piles of rocks marked old mills or house sites, whose pasture this had been where fifty-year-old trees now towered, and how many kids had been raised by whom in a long-gone log cabin beside this spring. He had accumulated this knowledge through his deep love of the mountains, the bright creeks, and their stream-bred trout.

It was Johnson who first pointed out to me the fading but still visible legacy of the narrow-gauge logging railroads. On almost every creek we fished — miles from dirt roads, often leagues from a paved road — he'd show me the evidence. The trails alongside the creeks were — and still are — graded trams or rail beds with regular impressions of cross ties often visible under leaves or moss. The ground in many spots is covered with coal, and it is not unusual to find railroad spikes or abandoned tools. Under dense rhododendron thickets, he showed me lengths of cable or other pieces of rusting equipment. I have caught trout in pools containing twisted rails that mark an era few are old enough to remember. Almost all of it is still there, and Johnson brought it to life for me. Like a new sponge, I sopped it up.

"They put the log purlins here, and the train would come up this gorge below us and cross the creek about there, then go on up that grade," he'd say, pointing out where timber cutters at the turn of the century had constructed a temporary crude log trestle to span a spring run or otherwise unnegotiable gap. I'd look at the steep terrain, the plunging pools, the trees growing up in the middle of the tram, and try to imagine a snorting locomotive hauling a steam donkey crane and cars full of virgin logs through this now-quiet paradise I had come to love.

Like most of today's casual visitors to our mountains, I was not then aware of what had once taken place in these isolated coves, and certainly not the extent of the intrusion. I knew that western North Carolina had been settled late, and that much of it lay untouched until after 1800, when settlers began to move up the creeks, build cabins, and carve out a meager existence. But their impact was marginal, and I could scarcely imagine the changes that had been wrought from the 1880s until the 1940s, when huge private timber companies systematically cut the virgin timber from virtually every mountain, cove, and creek bank.

If you walk these creeks and hills today, you will find the artifacts of that era along virtually every stream all the way to its headwaters. You will also observe that in the intervening years, young forests have again covered most of these once-barren hills.

Yet there is a lesson here, one that bears remembering. It is visible in many old photos of logging operations that show the mountains stripped to stumps. When a major hurricane stalled against the Appalachians in July 1916, it dumped twenty-two inches of rain at Altapass. With scant vegetation on many slopes to slow it down, a huge wall of water moved downstream washing out bridges and entire towns. The French Broad crested at twenty-seven and two-tenths feet at Blantyre, and washed away the gauge at Asheville when the water had already risen nearly fifteen feet above flood stage. In Caldwell County, Wilson Creek literally washed away the booming logging town of Mortimer, but Mortimer was by no means the only community to experience such a fate.

As severe as the damage was to human habitation, the 1916 flood was also disastrous to countless streams that had already been gravely damaged by the intense logging. Some streams would never recover their former native brook trout populations, and it has taken decades to wash out the silt. In 1940, two more floods struck that were nearly as devastating.

We tend to think of such events as natural disasters, but these floods hardly fit that description. Indeed, much of the damage was man-made, the result of uncontrolled timbering that had removed the forests capable of filtering the water and releasing it more gradually. Ironically, the floods created the opportunity for the U.S. Forest Service to acquire much of the land that comprises our western national forests, and they set the stage for restoration of the denuded hillsides.

Today, it is easy to judge those who clear-cut those virgin forests without thought to consequences, but it may not be fair to do so. Times and priorities were different then, and we are now more likely to manage our natural resources in light of what we have learned the hard way. We still make mistakes, and trout streams are still seriously damaged here and there by timber cutting, but the era of logging trains has passed.

You may thrill to their romantic past, as I do when I walk a trail where logging trains once ran, yet I am thankful that the forest is gradually erasing their memory.

The Laws of Discontinued Perfection

"You're going to buy another fly rod?" my friend exclaimed one day a few years ago as we were eating our sandwiches on the bank of a trout stream. "Just like the one you're using? Eye-dentical!?!"

I nodded in the affirmative.

"But why? There's nothing wrong with this one. Besides, you've already got half a dozen different brands of 7½-foot fly rods, not to mention heaven knows how many others in various lengths and weights. Some of them are high-dollar, too."

"How old are you?" I asked. He said he was twenty-four.

"Well, I guess you're too young to have run into the Law of Discontinued Perfection, but you will. You're right in saying that some of those other rods are okay, and a couple are very good, but it has taken me more than forty years of fishing to find a 5-weight, 7½-foot fly rod that I really, really like — one that's as delicate and light as a 3-weight, but with the power to punch a big Wulff into a stiff wind or roll a weighted Tellico nymph under overhanging rhododendron.

"Virtually no one makes fly rods specially suited for southern Appalachian streams, but now that I have finally found such a rod, two things are certain to happen under the Law of Discontinued Perfection. First, the company is going to quit making that particular rod. Then, within a few weeks of that executive decision, I'll slam this one in a car door. Or lose it. Or it'll get sent to Australia on a Ford Tri-Motor by some baggage clerk who thinks RDU stands for Really Down Under. It never fails, and as a result, forty years of personal research and experience will be shot to hell."

He gave me that look of immortal youth, the one reserved for the terminally anal retentive.

"Fortunately, there's a way to protect yourself," I continued. "If you ever discover any product that suits you perfectly, buy at least two of them. Get a dozen if you can afford them."

"Okay, so what if you break both rods?" he said. "You're right back where you started, and much poorer for it."

"Can't happen," I replied. "You're protected by the Second Law of Discontinued Perfection, which states that if you acquire an item in multiples, nothing will ever happen to the first one. As you get older, you'll learn to consider all those duplicates as a form of insurance, not to mention a priceless inheritance for your heirs."

"I think you've gone off the deep end," he said. "I'll bet you've got a case of Ipana toothpaste in your medicine cabinet."

"Didn't your mama tell you it's not polite to look in other people's medicine cabinets?" I said sternly. "Look, it isn't only fishing rods. For example, about fifteen years ago, I fell in love with a pair of padded wader socks called Bama Sockets. I wore them out, then learned they were no longer available. Called all over the country. No dice. Then, this past year, a friend found a supplier in Great Britain, so I ordered six pairs. I figure I'm set for wader socks until the end of the twenty-first century. I can name you hundreds of items—everything from worm hooks and casting reels to boots and guns—that you'd consider ideal for the task at hand, except you can't get them anymore. Why do you think high rollers are paying huge prices for reproduction Parker and Fox shotguns? The real thing ain't being made anymore."

My fishing buddy chewed his liverwurst and said nothing, but I could see I had gotten his attention. "I guess I do have a few things I would hate to be without," he mused. "This cap I'm wearing is the only dark green Daffy Duck fishing hat I've ever seen that was made of Gore-Tex. I would hate to lose it."

"See what I mean? You should have bought every one on the rack or written the factory and ordered a gross the moment you realized that was a good hat."

"Yeah, well I can see maybe buying two hats, but graphite fly rods are expensive," he said. "Seems to me you've got to draw the line somewhere."

"Hey, you're looking at a guy who once owned two used 1970 Mavericks with over a hundred thousand miles on them," I replied. "Back in the mid-1970s, I had figured out that I could buy thirty-six old Mavericks for the price of one entry-level new BMW, and I was planning to have enough $500 disposable fishing cars to last the rest of my life. Of course, they quit making Mavericks before I'd hardly got started."

We finished our sandwiches and began leapfrogging up the stream, fishing alternate pools. I even let my buddy try my favorite 7½-foot rod. He liked it and said he might even buy one someday.

He's too late. Six months after I bought my spare rod blank and stuck it in the closet as a hedge against the First Law of Discontinued Perfection, I got a call from my dealer.

"You know that little rod you ordered from me?" he said. "I think you got the last one. I just got word it's been discontinued."

Fishing and Supply-Side Economics

Is it just me, or does this sound familiar? One day this past summer, I needed to stock up on some lures and other tackle. I'd used up all my favorite colors of plastic worms and lizards, and a bass had run off with my favorite silver-finish topwater plug. My two best crawfish-colored crankbaits had found permanent homes in submerged stumps, and my last black muskie Jitterbug had inexplicably nested in the top of a forty-foot pine on a moonless night. I also wanted a particular brand of monofilament, a couple of dozen half-ounce reservoir worm weights, and some new skirts for my spinnerbaits.

I couldn't find a single one of those items in the almost identical tackle sections of four large chain stores, and my two favorite independent tackle shops had both recently gone out of business. I wasn't surprised. In recent years, it seems to be increasingly difficult for serious fishermen to purchase tackle. The large chain stores often don't carry what you need, and they've priced what they do manage to carry low enough to force many of the smaller independent shops out of business. Fishermen are the losers, of course, and it's at least partly our fault.

"I had to stop carrying fishing tackle," one local store owner told me. "I can't compete with the large chain stores. They're able to buy in volume and undercut my prices. The only way I might compete is to provide high-quality gear and specialty items and accessories that serious fishermen can't find in the chain stores. But I can't afford to buy and keep all that stock. Too many fishermen buy their lead weights and worms from me but go to the big chain stores to beat my prices on big-ticket items like reels."

It's certainly true that you can often find better prices at major chain stores, but with few exceptions, the selection is limited and largely geared toward midrange quality. Stocks are poorly planned and even more poorly maintained. Furthermore, when it comes to fishing knowledge, most clerks haven't got a clue, and even if they do, they have little control over what's in stock.

"Sorry, but we won't be reordering fishing tackle until early next spring," chain store clerks have told me on several occasions.

Typically, after April or May, plastic worms and lure selections have been picked over. On the other hand, if you want four dozen ultralight bubble-gum crankbaits, they've got 'em. The problem doesn't end with lures. Popular brands and sizes of line are likely to be long gone. That bristling rod rack is inviting until you take a closer look and find it contains dozens of nearly identical rods with little or no variety in length and action. Specialty items and accessories for serious anglers are seldom stocked. True, it isn't always so bleak in every store, but the situation I've described is fairly typical.

In most large chain stores, the orders for every store are apparently placed only once each winter by some national, bottom-line buyer in the distant home office who has little or no idea what anglers truly might need or want at local outlets across the nation. Thus, with few exceptions, a store in Michigan is likely to have virtually the same limited stock as a store in North Carolina or Florida or California.

Another closely linked trend is the rise in large retail mail-order tackle suppliers. Fly fishermen and, to a lesser extent, saltwater fishermen have always depended heavily on catalogs. Now, more and more serious anglers for bass, walleye, and panfish are also forced to buy by mail from Bass Pro Shops, Cabela's, and others. Yet while catalogs offer good prices, quick service, and better selections, they also pose a threat to local independent shops.

It's ironic. You'd think the rapid growth within the multi-billion-dollar sportfishing industry would result in greater availability of fine tackle on the local level, but that's not the case. Furthermore, manufacturers seem to be content with the present trend, and they may even be encouraging it.

Of course, there are still quite a few independent tackle shops in business, especially in smaller cities and towns. Some have wonderfully complete stocks. Some don't. But if we want them to stick around, we'd better support them even if it means paying a bit more for some items.

It would be a real pity if someday there were no local tackle shops. We'd miss the clutter, the snapshots of catches, the friendly banter with old friends, and tips passed on by clerks. Who's going to tell you what's biting and where? And what's it worth to actually see, compare, and test the tackle you're thinking of buying?

Besides, how many chain stores or mail-order houses will dip you a tub of crickets and a bucket of minnows, then wish you luck and mean it?

Fishing and the Theory of Relativity

Some fishermen prefer big water and burly fish, and they pursue their passion on massive lakes or the open sea. Other anglers prefer a more intimate setting — a small stream or lake where delicacy and finesse are paired pleasures and the size of the fish is relatively unimportant. The key word here is "relatively."

I know a fisherman who bought his nine-year-old son an aquarium as a birthday gift. Together they picked out the fish, some of which, by chance, happened to resemble tiny bluegills.

Inevitably, the father began to wonder if those fish swimming happily under the fluorescent light could be caught. The aquarium was not, after all, unlike a tiny pond with macro weed lines and structure. The notion would not go away. What if I built a miniature foot-long fly rod out of split cane, he wondered, and made a fly reel from a sewing machine bobbin? The line could be waxed string, the leader 8X nylon, and there are hooks available as tiny as size 28. In its own way, it could be challenging, and certainly convenient.

Given such musings, the father was not altogether shocked when he happened to walk into his son's room one evening and surprise him in the act of feeding his fish with a tiny ball of white bread dangling from a length of sewing thread. Like father, like son — the brotherhood of anglers.

Hand in hand with an obsession for fishing goes an obsession for water, and even the smallest trickle or pothole can have its attraction. After some forty years of fishing, I am learning to put this realization to good use.

I like to fish large impoundments for bass, and I suppose I always will, but I have also renewed an early passion for pond fishing. There is seldom any competition from other fishermen, which means you can fish slowly and deliberately without worrying that someone might pull in ahead of you. Your equipment needs are modest and inexpensive — a small boat and paddle or electric motor, and a handful of tackle.

I like to fly fish at dusk with deer-hair bugs or bait-cast with topwater lures, and both techniques are ideal for ponds. I've also learned another very important fact. You are likely to catch more bass in an hour or two of pond fishing than you would all day on a large lake. True, many of the bass may be small, but the rewards are more frequent, and your chances of catching a real lunker are better than you might think. Furthermore, if the bass don't cooperate, you can always swap your bass bug for a bluegill bug and be fairly certain of catching something. Fishing a pond carefully can be intensely delicious in ways that cannot be duplicated on a large lake. The same applies to other forms of angling.

Some years ago, the late Joe Brooks visited western North Carolina to fish some of our small trout streams. Brooks was a well-known book author and the angling editor of *Outdoor Life*. He had caught tons of big trout all over the world. Yet he was thoroughly enthralled with the challenges presented by the wild trout that populated the small stream he chose to fish.

Although most of the trout were less than eight inches long, he stalked them with obvious pleasure and displayed genuine admiration for a twelve-inch stream-bred brown he managed to fool. It was, he remarked, a more difficult fish to catch than the ten-pound brown trout he'd caught that year in Argentina. It was refreshing to hear him say that, and it confirmed something I had suspected for a long time. Bigger is not always better.

Years earlier, after a hitch with Uncle Sam, I had little money for fishing tackle, and none whatsoever for such big-budget items as boats. With few alternatives, I began wading the small, neglected streams of the Piedmont. I needed only an old pair of tennis shoes, an ultralight spinning outfit, and a handful of small spinners.

The shallow, rocky streams of Alamance and Orange Counties were canopied corridors of near-wilderness winding through rapidly developing areas, and they were seldom fished. It was not unusual to catch dozens of hand-sized robin, and occasionally there was a chance at a real trophy — a largemouth bass or pickerel that might go a couple of pounds.

Such fishing still exists in countless midstate streams, and the angling pressure remains light. Perhaps it's because too few fishermen understand the angler's theory of relativity as well as Joe Brooks. It's something I have tried to remember, but not always successfully. My memory is usually jogged, however, when I'm sitting fishless on a big lake under a blazing sun surrounded by water-skiers and other anglers.

The Summers before Air

We complain about the heat this time of year, but it could be just habit. With homes, malls, theaters, workplaces, and vehicles all air-conditioned, many of us don't spend ten minutes a day outside anymore. Everywhere we go, that ever-present hum holds the season at arm's length. Of course, those who haul irrigation pipe in tobacco fields or spread tar on roofs could tell us what we're missing, and no doubt would, given half a chance.

I suspect the development of air-conditioning has had more to do with the explosive growth and change in the Southeast over the past twenty-five years than anything else. But aside from that debatable merit, we'd probably vote to keep it.

Lately I've been getting reacquainted with the miseries and delights of summer—summer as it was in the early 1950s. My time machine is a three-room clapboard house that has been sitting abandoned and covered with vines in the middle of a field for as long as I can remember. I vaguely recall seeing children playing in that yard when I was a child, but that was over forty-five years ago. I don't know when it last had windows or doors, or if it had ever been painted.

Only wasps, dirt daubers, and a six-foot blacksnake lived there two years ago when, on a whim, I pushed through the catbriers, Virginia creeper, and cow itch and went inside. Scattered about were pieces of farm equipment and fertilizer sacks. The walls were unpainted pine but were basically intact, except where someone had fired buckshot through the open back door, leaving a nice pat-

tern beside the chimney. There were two rooms downstairs and a narrow stairway leading to a loft. The floors
were solid. As I stood in an open upstairs window and
looked out across the farm, a bobwhite whistled in the
hedgerow. What a wonderful place, I thought.

I continued to think about it as I drove home. Could be
a good getaway. No need for electricity or water. Might
add an outhouse later. Would need seven windows, two
doors, maybe a porch on the front. No, make that two
porches, front and back. A hammock swung on the back
porch would overlook the pond. Should check the tin
roof and flues. Wonder where I could find an old wood
cookstove? Buy wasp spray, I wrote on a notepad.

A few months later, it was basically finished and filling
up with castoff furniture. Aside from being a good fishing
and hunting camp, it has reminded me of just how little
we really need. And it has given me back my barefoot
summers.

"You can't stay there in July and August," I was warned.
"You'll stifle." I thought so too, but people who built
houses before air-conditioning considered such things as
cross-ventilation and orientation to prevailing winds. A
breeze is as reliable as the trade winds in these thermal-
sensitive fields, and the downstairs is often comfortable
even when the temperature is 95. In the early morning, it
is often cool enough for a light quilt. Even the heat from
the wood cookstove is tolerable from 4 A.M. until an hour
after sunrise, but it is easy to understand why lunches long
ago were often leftover breakfast biscuits and cold sweet
potatoes.

The body adjusts its thermostat. Washed in gentle airs
and unassaulted by humming fan or compressor, summer
reappears in the half-wakefulness of an afternoon nap.
You can feel it stirring the hair on your arms, hear it in the
top of the cedar where the mockingbird sits, or smell it in

the gardenia and sweet betsy outside the window. I dream of kin long gone, sitting on porches in cane-bottomed chairs, shelling peas into pans that rest on aprons across ample laps. I can hear the rattle of ice as the crank turns, and the water, milky with salt, pours from the drain on the side of the wooden tub. "Thee makes the best ice cream, Anna Mary," someone is telling my Quaker grandmother as we sit in the shade of a huge oak, waiting for our turn to lick the dasher.

A young boy in khaki shorts is walking up a sandy road beside a huge cornfield in the shimmering heat. He is carrying an air rifle in one hand and a twin orange Popsicle — sucked nearly white — in the other. The melt is dripping off a sticky elbow. At noon every day, he waits for the steam train to cross the road at the end of the field. The corn rattles lightly as he sits in a swarm of gnats.

I awake and sit up in a blind daze until I realize that I am not ten years old and no train is coming. Outside, the shadows are long, and Fowler's toads and bullfrogs are singing at the pond's edge. Soon the fireflies will gather their random sparks over the fields and the edge of the woods until thousands pulse together as though strung on wire. I have waited too long to fish, but no matter. Summer is ripe, and I need only move from the sofa to the hammock on the porch to continue the harvest.

Live Entertainment

We had fished a remote trout stream and hiked out a steep trail. The supper dishes were stacked, and the katydids and lightning bugs were preparing the evening's sound and light show. With no phone or TV in the tiny mountain cabin, I was anticipating a long evening of reading followed by the blissful sleep of the (presumed) innocent. I've learned, however, that the combination of a full belly and a book is premeditated slumber, so one more ritual seemed in order.

"I think I'll take a walk," I told Jack.

"Good idea," he said. In the gathering twilight, we meandered down the dirt path under a black canopy of hemlocks that glittered with bioluminescent bugs. At our feet, hovering fireflies cast eerie ovals of light on the road as though probing their way with tiny flashlights. Here and there through the trees, we could catch a glimpse of the nearby stream, the riffles shining faintly under a thin slice of moon. We walked toward the distant mercury vapor light in front of the old clapboard store. As we reached it, Jack suddenly stopped.

"Look at the size of that toad!" he exclaimed. "And that one over there. They're nearly as big as cantaloupes."

Not only were they huge, they also seemed perfectly comfortable with uninvited company. Both continued to hunt the grassy fringes alongside the store for insects drawn to the light. The largest had taken a position beside concrete blocks that supported the porch. It sat motionless much of the time until it spotted a mole cricket, moth, or other insect. Then it would turn its head and look directly at its target, perhaps even taking a hop in that direction if necessary. The toad's long, sticky tongue would gather the meal faster than we could see. Goodbye, cricket.

"This is great," said Jack, settling down for a lengthy stay. "Who needs public television when you can get a front row seat for the real thing? I'll bet those toads have been here for many years. No one bothers them, they've got a good home under the store, and there's almost never any traffic on this dirt road, especially after dark."

Shortly we were joined by a strolling family that found the show equally enthralling. Toad tales were shared. "When I was a kid, I used to roll lead shot down a board in front of feeding toads," confided one visitor. "Toads are attracted to movement, and they'd lap up every passing shot until they were too heavy to hop. Of course, we'd pick the toads up and pour out the shot, so I hope we didn't do them any permanent harm."

"Yeah, I remember doing the same thing," admitted Jack. "We also fed them lightning bugs—they love 'em—and after they'd eaten them, they would glow like Chinese lanterns."

"Do you suppose one of these toads would eat a meal this big?" I said, pointing out a mottled beetle over two inches long that had fierce-looking claws and a disposition to match. Jack probed the beetle with a stick, and it attacked aggressively. Jack placed the beetle in front of the largest toad. The beetle was still clinging to the stick with its claws and grasping a large piece of bark with its feet. The toad eyed it with interest.

"I'll bet he doesn't eat that," someone said.

With astonishing quickness, the toad lapped the beetle up, then daintily wiped the stick and bark off its chin with its toes. Inside the loose white skin of its throat, we could see evidence of a struggle.

"He can't stand that," said Jack. "He's sure to spit it out."

Our toad sat serenely like a diner at a late-night doughnut palace. Goodbye, beetle.

Back home, I consulted my toad references and learned some rather amazing facts about these common animals. Under favorable conditions, toads live a long time. Maximum age is unknown, but one captive toad lived to be thirty-six years old before it was killed accidentally. Toads must fill their stomachs four times a day, and they apparently limit their intake to anything that will fit, even bees, wasps, and spiders. Slugs are special treats. Toads are such effective pest controllers that they are often gathered and placed in gardens. According to one study, a toad can eat nearly ten thousand insects in three months. The two most common, and nearly identical, species found here are the American toad (*Bufo americanus*) and the southern toad (*Bufo lentiginosus*).

Toads don't drink; instead, they absorb water through their skins, and they seem almost to sigh and swell with pleasure when they settle down like a sponge in a puddle. You may have witnessed the enormous congregations of toads that are attracted to warm, wet highways during an evening summer rain. Once, returning from the beach with my kids, we encountered hundreds of toads hopping across the wet macadam. As I slowed down and began dodging, Scott offered a suggestion.

"I think you'd better turn on your frog lights," he said.

In the back seat, Susan groaned.

The Last Elk's Legacy

The antlers nailed above the door were huge, and my first thought was that the owner of that small mountain store must have hunted in the Pacific Northwest at some time in the past.

"Nope," he replied to my question. "Them horns come from a elk ra't cheer in North Carolina, but I don't know exactly when 'cause my grandpappy shot him."

I encountered those massive elk antlers years ago, and I knew that there might be a good story in them. I'd read that when John Lawson explored North Carolina in the early 1700s, he reported that both elk and woods bison could still be found here, although it is doubtful that he actually saw any. And even today the state is full of place-names that represent the only links to a lost wildlife heritage. There are places like Wolf Ford, Panther Branch, and Buffalo Run, not to mention at least two Elk Creeks and a handful of Elk Knobs, Elk Ridges, and many similar places. But elk in North Carolina in modern times?

Part of the mystery begins to unravel in the story of George Gordon Moore's game preserve, which was established at Hooper Bald in Graham County. Moore acquired the land in 1909 in return for his services in helping an English company buy a huge tract of virgin timberland in this region. Moore wanted to entertain wealthy friends, and he enclosed some 1,500 acres in 1911 and stocked two sections with four buffalo and fourteen European wild boar. Later, he added more buffalo and boar, along with six Colorado mule deer, nine Russian brown bears, twenty-five black bears, two hundred wild turkeys, and numerous ring-necked pheasants. There were also fourteen elk.

By the early 1920s, Moore had lost interest in his remote Hooper Bald preserve and sold it to his foreman, Cotton McGuire, for $1,000. Soon after, McGuire held a boar hunt for his friends. During that now-infamous hunt, the wild boar broke out of their compound, and their offspring are still running wild and have spread through parts of western North Carolina, northern Georgia, and eastern Tennessee.

As for the elk, many were sold to private individuals, and about twenty-five were bought in the mid-1920s by the North Carolina Game Division — a forerunner of today's North Carolina Wildlife Resources Commission. Some of these elk were released on Mount Mitchell, and others are likely to have been stocked elsewhere in the mountains. Even though the elk were huge — adults reached a thousand pounds or more — they apparently prospered for awhile despite hunting pressure. Much of this land was still wild, and the elk were adept at taking advantage of the thick cover.

It is known that some elk also remained in the area around Hooper Bald, where they were hunted, and one report indicates that the last one was killed by a Robbinsville man, although no date was recorded. Ed Waldroop of Franklin, who worked for the Wildlife Commission for thirty-six years, recalled that an elk was killed by the brother of a girl he was dating sometime between 1937 and 1940.

"I had heard that some boys from over at Tusquitee had run into an elk over at Nantahala while they were over there fishing and drinking white liquor," Waldroop told me. "They said their dogs had run it, but they couldn't get a shot. Not long after that, this girl told me her brother shot an elk that had come to a fodder or haystack to feed one day when there was snow on the ground. I figured it was the same elk, and it was the last one I heard of being shot."

Jim Todd, an attorney in Lenoir, told me that the late Bill Crump, who lived on a remote part of Wilson Creek in Avery County, had mentioned seeing elk as late as World War II—a story confirmed by the late Archie Coffey of Edgemont.

"They were there all right," Coffey told me a few years before he died. "I used to see them from a distance in groups of six or seven along Wilson Creek. In fact, some people were afraid to fish the creek because the elk would run them up a tree. They were more dangerous than deer.

"As best I can remember, those elk were stocked in here by the state after 1928 when deer were also put in here. For twelve years after those deer were stocked, the hunting season stayed closed and the elk population also grew. The elk were even getting in people's crops, and some of them were shot. I know of three elk that were trapped near the mouth of Lost Cove Creek in the 1940s and taken to Mount Mitchell to be released, but only one of them survived."

At least one elk was still in the Wilson Creek area as late as 1946 or 1947. After the war, Buddy Postell of nearby Roseboro stayed in an old cabin on Wilson Creek for awhile and told Jim Todd that early one morning he saw an elk chewing the bark off an old apple tree in the yard.

"I suspect that's true," Coffey said. "That cabin was built by Bill Crump's brother, Theodore. It was abandoned before the war, but it was still standing. Sometime after the war, a game warden in this area was walking through that area and heard something in that old cabin. When he went to look, he surprised an elk that had gone inside. That elk came out the front door so fast he broke off both his antlers—I guess he must have been about ready to shed them anyway."

And what happened to the antlers? "Well, Ray Sutton — that was the warden's name — brought them to me," said Coffey. "They're over my mantel right now."

A Kinship in Stone

The August sun was falling into the tops of the distant trees, and the last light bathed the fields in a warm glow. At the crest of the hill, I pulled off the dirt path, opened the car door, and stepped out of the artificial cool into 90-degree heat. These rolling fields have not changed in the more than forty years I have known them. I have hunted quail here with a grandfather and father and, more recently, a son and daughter.

With no particular goal, I walked between the tall to-bacco plants, kicking up grasshoppers that soared ahead toward a large field of corn that seemed to fold along the contours like some giant yellow quilt. Off to my right, a quarter of a mile beyond the path, I could see an aban-doned house shrouded in vines, its dark windows over-looking a good stand of soybeans that rimmed a small pond. In every direction, the view was familiar. My grand-father, dead since 1968, could walk the same row today and see nothing different. I think that would please him.

As I turned back toward the car and paused for a last look, I noticed a triangular shape next to my foot. I reached down, half expecting it to be a clod of dry dirt. But no, it was a bit more substantial, an ancient spear point of carefully crafted stone, with delicate side notches and serrated edges that came to a sharp point. I thought I recognized its type as a Palmer or Kirk, but it was so nearly dark by then that in order to see the shape better, I held it between my thumb and forefinger and raised it to the dying light. It was an act I recognized immediately as being symbolic — as symbolic as it was accidental.

No doubt, I was the first human being to pick up this bit of stone in at least seven thousand years. For me, it was a moment of almost overpowering kinship between all humans who have visited, used, profited from, and perhaps loved this particular small plot of land. There seemed little difference between a grandfather dead nearly twenty years and an Indian dead thousands of years. Or me, or those who would follow. I also realized why it was important for me to walk into the familiarity of that field and take pleasure in such continuity wherever I might find it.

That short incident came to mind again over a month later in what at first seemed an unlikely place. I had traveled east to the town of Columbia, capital of Tyrrell County. With a population of something like one thousand, it is the largest town in the county. (I think the second largest is Gum Neck.) I first saw Columbia when it had no paved streets, when the hotel there (now gone) got two dollars per night, and when to get there you passed a succession of junked cars marked "Eat at Carley's Cafe" for twenty miles in either direction on US 64.

Columbia was my kind of town, and Tyrrell County was a sportsman's dream all the way from Fort Landing, the Frying Pan, and Gum Neck on the Alligator River west through the pocosin and swamps to the eastern shore of Phelps Lake. Even with the passage of years and the threats of superfarms, peat mining, and massive logging, the area still retains a lot of its wild appeal.

So as we sailed out of Columbia down the Scuppernong River into Albemarle Sound, I was pleased to see that the shoreline of this handsome blackwater river still looked like the kind of place where you'd want to watch your step. In the middle of the sound, the wind fell out completely, as it invariably does when I go sailing. Indeed, the entire sound as far as you could see in any direction was calm ("slick ca'm," as they still say in certain areas along the coast).

We turned loose the sheets, let the boat drift, and jumped over the side. Around us in the water were the tiny stingless jellyfish some people call phosphors. They brushed lightly against our legs as we drifted on boat cushions. What reminded me of the spear point as I floated there was the sudden realization that I could not see exactly where sky met water in the distance. Indeed, unless I turned to look at the boat or my companions, I could not see anything man-made whatsoever. Here was one of the few places left in North Carolina where an Indian who had lived thousands of years ago might look around and see nothing unfamiliar.

For more than a month, I had thought of that spear point as a gift from the past, and a reminder that we are only temporary keepers of the land and water. Now, all at once, it also seemed like a warning.

Down and Dirty

Upon his return from a week-long fishing trip, one of my friends found his wife waiting for him in the yard with a garden hose, a tire brush, and a box of industrial-strength soap powder. "Well, I was still wearing the same clothes I left in, so I guess it was understandable," he said. "Had to peel my socks off with a putty knife. On the other hand, none of my fishing buddies found my personal habits repugnant."

Indeed! Could it be that he and his companions had ripened together until they all smelled like an August roadkill? Getting grungy beyond all imagination seems to be the special talent of fishermen, hunters and, especially, campers. The only other people who ever get that filthy are Marines in boot camp. The difference is that Marines don't love it.

Case in point. After two solid days of bass fishing last summer, Jack Avent and I loaded up and headed for home. We were sweaty, sunburned, and covered with mud, dried algae, fish slime, scales, motor oil, suntan lotion, and insect repellent. You could tell where we'd missed applying repellent, because those spots were bloody graveyards for countless mashed carcasses of mosquitoes and deerflies. We were every socialite's nightmare, and I must admit we sort of reveled in it.

"Boy, are we grubby," Jack said reverently. "My teeth feel like they've got little sweaters on them."

Compared to serfs in the Middle Ages, early explorers, or bums riding the rails, most folks today have no familiarity with real dirt. Few can even imagine the kind of patina a week in the woods can yield and have no appreciation for it.

Some years ago, we coaxed Mom into joining a family camping trip. After her tent was set up, she disappeared into it for about an hour. When I peeked in later, it looked exactly like her bedroom at home. The cot had been made up with clean, neatly tucked sheets, there was a throw rug on the floor, and a battery-powered lamp and alarm clock sat on a crocheted doily on a bedside stand. I feel quite certain she would have hung pictures of her grandchildren had she been able to drive a nail in canvas. Later that evening, she sat around the campfire in a quilted robe and bedroom slippers. She accepted our kidding with befitting grace, and in all fairness, I think she had a grand time.

Those of us more accustomed to outdoor living are quicker to bend any rules regarding personal hygiene and fuel intake. For example, you would never dream of eating something you dropped on a spotless kitchen floor, but a hot dog that squirts out of your roll and falls into the mud can be wiped on a sleeve and safely consumed.

There's a story that a cowboy was once asked why he put so much pepper on everything he ate. "That way," he replied, "I don't have to wonder what all those little black specks are."

My pickiness as a child ("brat" is probably more accurate) became part of family legend the day I slept through an afternoon nap with a green pea in my mouth rather than swallow it. As an adult, however, I will routinely scarf a raw turnip picked up in a field, or eat soybeans straight off the stalk. Just this past spring at Mattamuskeet, I ate two ham sandwiches that I retrieved from the bilge of the boat, where they had been awash in half an inch of gasoline. Well, it *was* unleaded.

Some of us develop this tolerance early, in Scouts,

when the only thing you really try to remove from your food is something still moving. One fellow in our troop found worms in one end of a coconut candy bar, but he still ate the other end. His dog ate the rest. Waste not, want not. It was also as Scouts that we learned to wash mess kits with sand and river water, and that knives and forks required only a perfunctory wipe on your pants. In our troop, anybody caught washing his face, combing his hair, or changing clothes was branded a sissy.

When I was a kid, one of my favorite places in all the world was a ramshackle cabin built on pilings above a marsh in the mouth of the Little Alligator River near Fort Landing. It was no place for the fastidious. From all evidence, the kitchen shack must have literally been privy to every rat in Tyrrell County. What little washing we did was in the rain barrel that collected water from the roof, and after a few days, your skin developed a glaze that not even a salt marsh mosquito could penetrate. It was wonderful.

As we get older, most of us grow less tolerant of such conditions. We spend a fortune on soap, deodorant, toothpaste, and shampoo, and few of us are comfortable if we don't get a daily shower. Yet, think about the best times of your life. I'll bet you've been socially repulsive during most of them. In good company, soap is optional.

Bird Thou Never Wert

This is the time of year when mourning doves threaten to take over life on earth as we know it. You wake up in the morning, and there are half a dozen perched on the foot of the bed and several more picking up grit in the hall. One sits on the toothbrush rack and watches you shave.

Power lines look like strings of pearls sagging with beak-to-beak doves. Doves are begging bread crumbs in the malls and city squares, and they have reached such a state of obesity that they can barely waddle out of your driveway to keep from being run over. Throughout the land, the mournful voice of the turtledove swells to a chorus that would make the Mormon Tabernacle Choir sound like kids at Vacation Bible School.

Those of us who wait patiently for this time of year are wise to all this shameful duplicity. We know what's about to happen as well as the doves do, and brother, it ain't what they'd have you think.

If you read the fine print in Mother Nature's manual, you will discover a clause that explains this sudden deluge of doves. Under "Standard Dove Operating Behavior" are these instructions: "Appear ubiquitous in August; disappear in September. It drives hunters nuts. To determine the exact day of disappearance, consult local hunting regulations for the opening date of the season." I have filed all this under "Suspicions Confirmed."

Of course, every dove hunter is familiar with the mourning dove's taunting omnipresence prior to the season and sudden scarcity when the season opens. Nor does it help to know that doves are so prolific that their numbers have never been higher and may even be increasing. Ornithologists tell us that this sudden annual exit is not a mystery. They say the birds are simply so keyed into weather changes and migration patterns that the slightest cold snap or wet weather can push whole legions south overnight — usually on the evening before opening day. (Okay, so where the heck are those legions to the north of us that should be arriving here? Don't they have cold snaps up there?)

Experts have had less success explaining weight loss and conditioning in doves. How, for example, can a dove that is so roly-poly it can barely hop over a curb on the last day of August manage to achieve supersonic flight by Labor Day? All I know is that it's hard to believe there is any relationship between the corpulent creature vacuuming seeds at my bird feeder and the Mach II missile that comes in at twelve o'clock high over cut corn and pines a few days later. What transforms doves from pullet to bullet? Do they go to aerobic dancing classes, or what?

Even under ideal conditions, the dove hunter is at a greater disadvantage than you might suspect. If you can imagine what it might be like to spray a low-flying P-51 Mustang with a garden hose, you've got a pretty good idea of the odds on any given shot.

On the other hand, if you can bag enough doves for a meal, you're in for a treat. Over the years I have managed this feat just frequently enough to pass along accolades for dove breasts wrapped in bacon and roasted over charcoal. I can also attest to the edibility of a casserole of boned dove breasts baked with bread crumbs, sour cream, sage, sliced green peppers, chicken broth, and sherry.

For those not yet initiated, I should explain that there is a traditional way to hunt doves in North Carolina. You start with a 140-pound pig, a portable pit-cooker, five gal-

lons of coleslaw, corn on the cob, a foothill of hush pup-
pies, and washtubs full of iced-down watermelons. After a
midday porkout, the hunters who have not opted for a
nap take up positions around a large, likely field. If all goes
normally, waves of doves will begin to fly in to feed, with
the flights becoming larger and more numerous as the
afternoon progresses. The theory is that you need enough
hunters to keep lots of doves moving, but one bird can be
more than aplenty at times. I once counted twenty-two
missed shots at a single dove that darted unscathed across
a thirty-acre field, circled a few pines, then decided it was
safe after all. As astonished shooters watched, it fluttered
back into the field, pulled up a stool, put on a bib, and had
itself an ear of corn.

The hunts I remember best, however, have been ordi-
nary by most standards and uncrowded by choice. One
took place nearly thirty years ago, with my grandfather,
father, and brothers. We sat on stools in the shade of a
magnificent walnut and took turns kidding each other
about our dismal shooting skills. On another occasion,
Mike Gaddis and I built a blind of corn shucks on a crisp,
bright day during the second half of the season and let his
superb Labrador retriever, Squaw, do most of the work.
We knew doves were coming when Squaw shivered, and
she dutifully retrieved Mike's limit, along with several that
happened to be in the wrong place when I shot.

Most of all, perhaps, I remember the Indian summer
afternoon I had a field all to myself and spent most of it
watching huge, puffy clouds sail past like clipper ships. I
didn't fire a shot, but dreams were in the wind, and a dove
casserole was home in the freezer.

The Last, Best Day

From the top of the big rock on the ridge, you can look west across the valley to the tall mountains. At this distance, they are a hazy lavender. Since 1967, when I first discovered this spot, it has been a late October ritual to stop here for a few moments before following the long, steep trail down to the trout stream.

If you lie on the rock and look straight up into the rising circle of maples and hickory, the brilliant Indian summer sky will be framed in scarlet and gold. When there is no wind to lightly rattle the leaves, there may be absolute silence — the kind that makes you strain to hear anything above a faint rush in the inner ear. That moment of utter stillness helps me recalibrate my senses for what has often been the finest day of the year.

Back on the trail, I follow steep switchbacks down the mountain through dense rhododendron thickets and into sunless coves where springs seep across mossy boulders. At spots the trail is nearly knee-deep in leaves, and their rhythmic swish keeps time for an old bluegrass song that has come to mind: "I'd rather be in some dark hollow, where the sun don't never shine . . ."

Fifty-five minutes later I can hear the rush of water, and I soon break out into the flats, where the ferns have already turned yellow. They seem almost luminous in the filtered light beneath the canopy of towering hemlocks and tulip poplar. Just beyond is a house-high rock that slopes down to the stream. The water is low and clear, as I had expected. At the base of the rock is a deep pool, an emerald strung by threads of whitewater to a necklace of shallow amber pools above and below.

A small trout is trapped in amber just upstream. I see its shadow on the gravel, then the fish itself as it hangs there, moving slightly up and down to inspect offerings too tiny for me to see. Then it rises deliberately and sips something from the surface.

Quickly, I remove my hiking boots, hide them under a rhododendron, then lace up the felt-soled wading shoes I've been carrying. In a few moments, the small Wulff Royal is knotted to the leader, and I stoop low and ease down the rock until I am about thirty feet behind the trout. It takes the fly eagerly.

The first fish is always a confirmation of sorts. This stream, its watershed, and its trout are so unspoiled that I keep expecting to arrive and find it has all been a dream. Or worse, that it was not a dream, but a treasure pillaged while I was away. Or worse yet, that I will have to endure a patient and paternalistic explanation for its loss. It doesn't take much to spread sand and silt miles downstream — a road bulldozed through the headwaters, a clear-cut on the steep slopes, or a few misplaced mountain chalets. The threat is not fantasy. Two nearby streams in this national forest have recently been crippled, and another has been so severely choked with sand from a new logging access road that it will not recover in my lifetime.

But this little trout, just released, hovers over reassuringly clean rocks, its golden flanks and random red spots revealing a sure lineage to the German browns that were first stocked here in the late 1800s to replace the diminished native brook trout that once held dominion.

A mile upstream, I find my favorite mossy glade beside the stream and take off my vest. A familiar rock forms a perfect backrest. Beside it, a second rock has just the right shape to cradle a drink while I eat a ham sandwich. In nearly three decades, only one major tradition has been abandoned. Once I would have eaten a liverwurst, onion, and ripe Liederkranz cheese sandwich, but I learned by experience that retribution was too swift. The postlunch nap, however, is still observed.

By late afternoon I have lost count of the trout I've caught and released, but all the likely chutes and pockets have yielded at least a strike. Most of these trout are small, but it is not unusual to catch — or, rather, see — bigger fish. I am looking at one now.

It lies in only a few inches of water at the tail of a long pool where an almost imperceptible side-current slides alongside a grassy, undercut bank. A mere flick of the tail, and the trout can swap kitchen for bedroom.

What to do? The trout hasn't seen me, but I am too exposed to risk retreat and mount a possibly more effective approach. Yet if I try to cast from here, the trout will surely see the movement of my arm or the fly line. I stand motionless for what seems a long time. A light breeze momentarily ripples the water, and I use that advantage to sink to a kneeling position.

I take a deep breath, false cast over the open part of the pool where I hope the trout won't notice, then angle the cast so that the fly lands several feet above the trout. The fly floats past the spot. I try again. Then again. Nothing. I slowly stand and take a look. The trout is gone.

On the rock at the top of the trail, I sit until the far mountains are lost in darkness and the sky is vaporous with stars. The warmth of the day is long gone, but a little lingers on the surface of the rock, and I will carry just enough of it home with me to survive the winter.

Shooting with Bone-Narrows

No one seemed to be home when I stopped by a friend's house one recent afternoon, but I kept hearing strange noises from around back. Ping, thunk. I walked through the hedge and found Joe standing on one side of the yard shooting arrows at a target he'd mounted in front of a steep embankment.

"I didn't know you were an archer," I said.

"Well, some of the people I shoot with have made the same observation," he said, chuckling. "But to tell the truth, I've been at it for about two years now, and it's one of the most absorbing hobbies I've ever had. Mostly I've been target shooting, but this year I'm figuring on trying to get a deer."

"One with suicidal tendencies, I would guess," I kidded.

"Without question," he agreed, "but it won't be because I'm short of gear."

He had aluminum arrows and a state-of-the-art compound target bow — one of those funny-looking jobs with wheels and wires. It was mounted with an elaborate sight, and on the string near the nocking point was a button he called a kisser. "You draw the bow until the button hits your lips at the same spot each time you shoot, and it helps you get the same draw and hold each time," he said. "Archery is a pretty sophisticated sport these days."

I'll say it is. I had a pretty rampant case of "bone-narrow" fever when I was a kid, but I haven't shot a modern bow like Joe's more than a few dozen times. Perhaps no sport associated with hunting or fishing has undergone more major innovations in equipment in the past thirty years than archery. You can still recognize and use the guns and fishing gear you grew up with, but if you handed a 1950s archery buff a modern bow, he might not know what it was.

My father, William Graham Dean, carried a boyhood interest in archery well into adulthood, and when I was old enough to shoot with him, he gave me a straight lemon-wood target bow with a twenty-pound pull. You couldn't buy a recurved bow then, although history books were full of illustrations of recurves used in ancient times. Thirty years ago, virtually all bows were straight and made of hickory or lemonwood. The best were probably made of yew or Osage orange. Dad's two bows were powerful, six-foot longbows (of Robin Hood fame), with real horn tips. He made them from blanks, one of lemonwood and the other Osage orange. Sadly, I broke the orange bow trying to string it, but I believe Dad has forgiven me. It's been long enough by now.

We ordered our supplies from L. E. Stemmler in Man-orville, New York, a company that apparently bit the dust just before archery became a boom industry. I still re-member poring over those old catalogs looking at Port Oxford cedar arrow shafts, feather fletching, and leather finger guards. Even today, I never smell beeswax without thinking of waxing a flax bowstring.

Of course, modern archery gear is superior in many ways, but it would be a mistake to assume that a wooden longbow like my father's wasn't a lethal and accurate weapon. Unless you used a leather arm guard, it would peel the skin from elbow to wrist, and it took real strength to draw and hold it. It was also a flat-shooting son-of-a-gun, and it was no surprise to me when Howard Hill took his longbows to Africa in the 1950s to film the classic big-game hunting film *Tembo*. Hill bagged virtually every ma-

jor species, including Tembo (elephant), with a longbow.
Of course, you won't see that film in any theater again.

As for me, I hunted mostly cardboard boxes. I'd stack
them up in the backyard and stalk them from behind
trees or shoot them Indian-style as I raced past hanging
from the neck of my pinto pony. That's the way I saw it,
anyway. If you'd been watching, you would have seen
some grimy little kid in short khaki pants straddling a
stick.

I learned a few things about archery from those early
years. First, don't shoot on a grassy lawn, because arrows
burrow so completely you can't find them. Second, you
don't need a target as big as a cardboard box after you get
your "eye" and shoot instinctively. I could pick off bottle
caps by the end of that summer. Finally, and most important, don't shoot straight up.

Once, at the edge of a field, I let a neighborhood kid
shoot my bow, and before I could say anything, he aimed
straight up and let fly. We watched the arrow go out of
sight, and then it occurred to us that we had no idea
where it would come down. I could suddenly see myself
shish-kabobbed from top to bottom, and you've never
seen kids scatter so quickly. We never found the arrow.

Later on, Dad gave me a solid glass recurved bow, but it
never shot quite the same as the old lemonwood bow, and
although I tried to shoot some squirrels with it in the
woods behind my grandmother's house, I never hit anything. I guess I really didn't want to shoot a squirrel with
an arrow, anyway — I just liked the idea of hunting something more wary than a box.

Those memories came back a few weeks ago when I was
in my parents' attic and saw Dad's old longbow hanging
on two nails. I also recalled that once when I was very sick,
he had read me his favorite book, *Robin Hood.* At the end
of the book, when he lay dying, Robin asked his friend

Little John to hand him his bow so that he could shoot one last arrow. His last wish was to be buried where that arrow landed. I always liked that notion, but you can bet when my time comes, I won't shoot straight up. Who's in any hurry?

The Art of Anticipation

For several days last winter until I got around to cleaning them, the rear and side windows of the family vehicle were so badly smeared that they appeared to have been licked. Which they had.

The drool in question belonged to a pointer named George — affectionately and accurately nicknamed The Bonehead by his owner, Andy Aretakis — and it had been deposited liberally on the windows en route from Raleigh to Wilmington. Until that trip, I had honestly thought that I was the only soul who mentally hunted fields as I drove through the countryside. Turns out, George also hunts while riding. I've never seen a dog cover so much ground in a backseat, or so much glass with a nose. He even pointed twice at 55 miles per hour, once near Spivey's Corner and again somewhere south of Clinton.

Though George's two-hour stint of snuffling, quivering, and rapid rear-seat transit tended to be distracting at times, I had no trouble understanding. It's perfectly obvious that the ol' Bonehead is a master of anticipation, and he shares that trait with his biped companions. And as is so often the case, anticipation was the better part of George's trip, which is another way of saying that we probably should have checked out his flying points, since the actual hunt produced none.

I have observed over the years that anticipation is the better part of a lot of trips, if not the majority of them. Indeed, the wide gap between hope and fulfillment is probably the best argument for our inability to foresee the future. How many hunting and fishing trips — how much of life itself—would you have scrapped if you'd known in advance how things would turn out?

Most of us have endured a long history of fishless fishing trips and birdless hunting trips, some of which could not possibly have lived up to our expectations. I am especially mindful of the many times my father and I trusted our fortunes to his old pointer Buck, the original "Pointer of No Return."

Buck had an uncommon instinct, even among his breed, to determine exactly where we were at all times and studiously avoid us at all costs. We spent a lot of time hunting, of course, but mostly hunting for Buck. All dogs may go to heaven, as is commonly believed, but I would be greatly surprised if Dad passed through the Pearly Gates and found Buck locked on a covey. It would be far more characteristic if, on that day, Buck were contentedly prowling through the lowlands along the River Styx. Still, I must admit that we thoroughly enjoyed those hunts up until the very moment we actually began.

Buck, of course, can hardly be blamed for other occasions of unforeseen destiny. Had I but known several winters ago what lay ahead of us on a duck-hunting trip to the Little Alligator River, I would have immediately canceled the trip and gladly spent that time reading Milton's *Paradise Lost.* The highlight of that trip—is there such a term as "lowlight"?—was the overturning of a brand new truck in a marsh. Close behind was the food poisoning that overtook various members of the party at inopportune moments. No moment, by the way, is more inopportune than when you are dressed in half a dozen layers of goose down and chest waders at dawn in a remote duck blind on a 10-degree morning.

Finally, there was the anticlimactic moment when a duck—the only duck anyone saw in three days—buzzed our decoys. This suicidal gadwall flew unscathed through a barrage on the left side of the blind, then circled widely and made a run at us from the right, where it was promptly missed by the very gunners who were in the act of jeering the left-hand battery. An equal opportunity duck, it flew off leisurely and plopped down just out of range, where it dabbled happily for the remainder of the morning.

Despite the misfortunes that befell us on this trip, I should probably note that the hunt also provided one other unforgettable moment. As we sat in the blind one morning, a gray stillness fell over the marsh and the dark, ice-fringed water. The decoys sat motionless on perfect reflections, and all the colors around us faded to a luminous silver just as the snow began to fall. We sat in almost total silence, hearing only the faint tick of ice crystals striking the grass and the mingled two-note songs of three magnificent swans that passed overhead.

The life of a hunter and fisherman — perhaps all life — is like that. The unpleasant moments are largely unavoidable, but so are the unexpected moments of delight. You cannot plan them, nor would you truly want to. The topwater strike of a largemouth bass; the appearance of a large buck at the edge of the woods; pintails swinging into the decoys — all are enhanced by their unpredictability.

Dad told me once that as I grew older, it would become more and more difficult for me to convince myself to make the effort to go out. The packing, early mornings, long drives, and uncertainties would more easily prevail. "But go anyway," was his advice. "Make the effort if you possibly can. You never know what will happen."

No, but you can look forward to it anyway.

Calling All Dogs

When it came to naming dogs, my grandfather was of the practical persuasion. Since all his dogs were trained to hunt, point, and retrieve bobwhite quail, he chose easily understood, one-syllable monikers. Frank and Mack were the first I remember. They were standard, business-model bird dogs that generally reflected the direct and honest qualities of their master. Because their names were simple, both the dogs and the owner could keep them straight.

But as the years rolled by, there came a steady succession of dogs. Chief followed Frank and Mack, then Sam took a brief turn. After my grandfather's death, Dad owned several dogs, including Mack II and Buck. When Buck finally went to that great peafield in the sky, a puppy named Jake was already coming along nicely. All this while, we were hunting steadily with good friends who likewise carried a line of one-syllable dogs who answered to names like Mutt, Pat, and Meg.

In the long run, we were undone by the rule of simplicity. It is easy enough for a dog named Buck to remember his name, but not so easy for his owners and handlers, who have to sort through forty years of dogs and a legacy of two dozen similar names while bobwhites are blowing out wildly from underfoot and the monosyllabic dog of the moment is approaching orbit.

Far too often I have shouted "Mo, Muck" when I really meant "Whoa, Buck." Or Mack. Or Mutt. Needless to say, Muck never paid any attention whatsoever, and I can't say I blame him.

So I listened with considerable interest when Vic Venters reported that a trainer of his acquaintance from Richlands names all of his female dogs Lady, and has done so for years.

"He never mangles a name or has to fumble through half a century of bloodlines to get to the right one," Vic explained. "And those dogs don't know whether the Lady being summoned is a daughter, sister, or grandmother. They're all Ladies."

I have heard of yet another gentleman who has devised an even better system. Every living creature on his place is named Buck. All his dogs are named Buck. His wife is named Buck. His sons and daughters are named Buck. His mules — both Buck (no doubt). His cows, hogs, goats, and chickens all answer to Buck. When someone asked him why he had gone to such extremes, he was quick with the answer.

"Because, by gum," he said, "when I call, I want something to come a-running."

Not everyone seeks simplicity in naming a dog, and that certainly applies to line-bred field trial dogs. Some titles string together more heirloom family cognomens than the last seed of Virginia aristocracy. Champion Mississippi Zev and Champion Johnny Crockett are among the most celebrated field trial bird dogs of all time, but while their performances on the ground might be unmatched, they have somewhat pedestrian names compared to many other trial dogs. I once saw a dog named Hightone's Rapid Rip run in a local trial, and I thought it carried an inspired arrangement of appellations. Who among us has not called that dog a time or two?

Nor are English pointers and setters the only canines who sport extended, weighty titles. In a recent beagle trial magazine, I noted dogs with such names as Gundog Allen's Boogy-Woogy Banjo, Daniel's Cane Cutter Cody, and

Bryson's Swamp Creek Buzz Boy. Of course, such titles usually denote lineage, and handlers adopt shorter nicknames to handle packs of beagles in the field. Imagine the confusion if full names were required. It would take a week to get all the tangs untongled.

Of course, those of us who also own countless pets, mixed-breed mutts, and hearth-bound gundogs aren't always governed by hunting tradition or lineage. We more often pick names based on whimsy. Folks in our office own dogs named Muldoon, Watson, Weenie, and Manfred, although there is one Rover. (A few fierce traditionalists remain.) But I haven't run across a dog named Spot in years, and one recent poll notes that Pepper is now the most popular name for a dog. We once owned a shorthair appropriately named Pepper because of its densely speckled color, but some people apply the same name to pure white poodles. White Pepper? Is there such a thing as a gastronomically correct dog?

Which reminds me that I once acquired part ownership of a poodle in a package deal. A more miserably neurotic dog never lived, but I think I know why. How would you like to go through puppyhood with a name like Dior? If it had been left up to me, I'd have called him Buck.

The Thanksgiving Hunt

My young friend Duffy has never had a real Thanksgiving. That's my uninvited opinion, by the way. He doesn't even call it Thanksgiving. It's turkey day to him, and the title seems to fit. Duffy sleeps until late morning, and along about midafternoon, he eats corn-oil-implanted turkey breast, canned yams, boil-in-the-pouch veggies, a chunk of congealed cranberry sauce, some brown-and-serve rolls, and heat-and-eat pumpkin pie. His guests are the teams from the National Football League. After dinner, he is lulled to sleep on the floor in front of the TV by dulcet voices describing a 35-to-3 nail-biter. He never goes outside and may not even look out the window.

Actually, I have experienced some of Duffy's turkey days and moderately enjoyed them, but let me tell you how I remember Thanksgiving when I was growing up in eastern North Carolina in a family rich with traditions.

I recall the way it felt early Thanksgiving morning to be packed into Granddad's blue Buick with the dogs in the trunk and Dad kidding us about the birds we were going to miss. I was old enough to carry a shotgun, but my younger brother carried a BB gun just as I had done before him. We were always carefully instructed on the safe handling of guns, but it was not so much dogma as it was a proper ritual to be passed down. Like a family Bible, it was an inheritance.

We walked the fields behind the dogs, and we always wanted to find a covey tight in the broomstraw in the middle of a field the way the calendars showed it. We rarely

THE THANKSGIVING HUNT 113

did. Our birds were largely woods birds then — just as they are now — which makes me wonder whether we remember the real hunts or just the calendars. The dogs would nearly always find birds in the dense bottoms of honeysuckle and volunteer pines. We would wade through the mess, and I would miss the shot because the birds would get up just as I was trying to thread the barrels of the Sterlingworth through the greenbriers.

I don't remember that we killed many quail, or that it mattered. What I recall is the smell of crushed pine in the bottoms, and the winter sun in a faded sky. I remember the way the dogs looked as they rimmed a field, stark white against the brown. I recall the arrowheads I found and the dense bed of running cedar that was in the woods behind the tobacco barn. I remember the well and the cold water we drank from the enameled dipper.

But except for one bobwhite, I hardly recall shooting at all. We were behind a long-abandoned tenant house, and one of the dogs pointed at the edge of a soybean field. Because I was the youngest that day, I was awarded the honor of flushing the covey. Every bird in the bunch crossed to the right in front of my dad, so I had no shot. Except one bird. This quail got up late and went left, disappearing for a moment behind the rusted hulk of a '49 Mercury, then reappearing just at the edge of the pines for a brief moment, where I caught up with him and dropped him cleanly with a load of No. 8s. No one else had shot at this bird, or even seen him. It was the first time I'd ever been absolutely certain that no one else held an option. My bird. All mine. I celebrated by eating a double handful of soybeans to tide me over.

Along about noon, we would head home and wash up for the trip to Grandmother's. I'm not going to belabor this any more than necessary, because I don't want any readers starving to death, but if you've never had a scratch-made Thanksgiving dinner in rural Northampton County or some such place, you're poorer for it. Only a dozen or so grown folks could sit at the main table, while all the kids sat at smaller side tables. Even so, there was room on the main table for only one or two turkeys, smoked ham, fresh ham, and several kinds of stuffing. There would be at least twenty-five dishes of vegetables, casseroles, fruit salads, and hot rolls on the buffet. Just so you can get some idea of the magnitude, there would likely be half a dozen potato dishes alone. In addition to mashed potatoes, boiled new potatoes, and potato salad, there would be candied yams, a sweet potato casserole with raisins and marshmallows, young sweet potatoes in butter, sweet potato bread, and possibly sweet potato pie. Believe me, I am not kidding, and I'm quite certain I've overlooked at least a couple more potato dishes (but not French fries; they were virtually unheard-of). It's a wonder the table legs didn't collapse.

I have a vivid memory of standing at the end of the long counter in the kitchen and sighting down a row of eight hot mincemeat pies bolstered on the rear by half a dozen coconut, chocolate, and pound cakes and flanked on the front by plates full of roasted pecans, stuffed dates, and butter mints. There was no room in the dining room for desserts until everyone had eaten the main courses, and no one ever ate more than a pilfered pecan or a sliver of ham until the blessing was said.

Of course, Duffy could have such a Thanksgiving today. Some North Carolina families do, and hunting is sometimes still part of it. But I'll have to admit, it takes at least a father and a son — and if possible, a grandfather — to do the hunting justice. It also takes a passel of aunts, mothers, and grandmothers to make those table legs quiver. Not everybody has been so lucky as I have in that regard. Poor Duffy and his football Thanksgiving. Maybe now he will understand why I never call it turkey day.

Dogs Are a Better Class of People

My brother's Labrador retriever is beginning to get more than a little gray around the muzzle, prompting the suggestion that we might need to get him some Grecian Formula for all that grizzled foliage so that he can keep up appearances. It's the least we could do for our old buddy. After all, when the heat's on, having an unresponsive love interest would surely be a bitch. Unfortunately, dye can't hide the fact that John's grand old dog is winding down a career that has been an essential part of many memorable moments in duck blinds, boats, and marshes across North Carolina.

How can you not love a dog that shells his own peanuts in the blind, and once guarded a bunch of black walnuts for days while trying to figure out how to gain entrance? How many dogs do you know that like raw oysters? Okay, but with horseradish and ketchup? Then there's the time when cash crossed palms because, against all bets, John's Lab ate a pickled beet. Liked it, too.

What I will always remember best, however, is a hunt a dozen years ago when this then-youthful dog refused to give up on a crippled Canada goose. The goose was only slightly injured, and it quickly gained the cover of a swamp several hundred yards across a frozen impoundment. We figured we'd have to get it on the way out, but my brother's Lab ignored all orders, whistles, screams, and threats. He lunged against the rafts of ice, breaking a ragged trail across the impoundment and finally disappearing into the woods.

Time dragged, and we were beginning to think we had

a lost dog when suddenly the binoculars revealed a black speck on the distant dike. After pausing a moment, the Lab plunged in and began to break ice carrying a heavy and not altogether cooperative load. I still have the photograph of John's dog covered with rime, his paws on the last shelf of ice in front of us, proudly delivering that goose. Physically, he couldn't do that today, but I'll bet his heart would make him try.

Every breed — indeed, every individual dog — has characteristics that seem particularly human. Like people, some dogs seem to have a sense of humor, while others develop qualities that mirror the interests and character of their owners. Surely John Rucker's remarkable springer spaniel, Barney, shared his owner's love of fishing. The only time I was privileged to meet Barney, he and John were fishing for trout on the Smith River. If, in Barney's opinion, John was not catching enough fish, Barney would look elsewhere along the river for rising trout. Then he would encourage John to follow him. "Try these down here," I could imagine him thinking. "You've already spooked those up there with all that sloppy casting. By the way, they're taking size 24 blue-wing olives." And like his owner, Barney practiced catch-and-release, clamping the trout he retrieved so gently they could be turned back unharmed.

Yet almost all dogs, like children, can be supremely frustrating. My dad's lovable old pointer Buck has gone to that great peafield in the sky, but during his terrestrial tour, he loved to hunt bobwhites better than he loved leftover liver. The only problem is that he preferred to hunt them alone. We were never certain whether this was simply because he wanted to compensate for our disability (having only two legs), or whether he thought we tended to get in the way when birds were found. The result was that for a dozen years or so, Buck hunted birds and we hunted Buck. Yet, toward the end of his life, he mellowed and sometimes even stayed in the same county so that we could occasionally share in his great adventure. We did, of course, until his time was up. We still miss him fiercely.

Buck was followed by a setter named Jake who has managed to maintain puppyhood for fourteen years — no small achievement in itself. Unlike Buck, Jake actually likes for us to accompany him on the hunt, and in keeping with his uncommon consideration for others, he believes in equal opportunity for all species. Thus, he will point a sparrow, box turtle, or housefly with the same intensity that he might lock up on a bobwhite or timberdoodle. "You trained me to point, so I'm pointing" seems to be his credo. Say what you will, it keeps us on our toes, and Jake never lies. That's a fly, all right. Good boy.

In dog years, which is the way I prefer to keep count these days, I am only about seven years old, but my muzzle is already more than a bit grizzled, and I've had enough experience with dogs to wonder about one thing. Was it simply an oversight that humans were given a life span of seven or eight decades, and dogs got just a bit more than one? The only thing I can figure is that this sad disparity must be part of the plan. Otherwise, sensible men and women seeking only the highest qualities in a mate would surely have chosen dogs.

Birds out of Hand

We crossed the big field, snagging our boots now and again on wiry runners of brier and honeysuckle hidden beneath the dead grass and broomstraw. Ahead, we saw Meg momentarily in the opening under the big oak that stood in Estore's yard. Or rather, it would have been Estore's had he not been dead forty years and his frame tenant house abandoned. His face couldn't be called up by anyone still living on the farm — or perhaps anywhere else on earth — but in the peculiar ways that places are tagged, Estore has stayed to watch over the old tin-roofed house, with its sagging porch, tilted lightning rods, shaggy blue cedars, and sentinel oak.

Meg, we knew, would be checking out the smaller bean-field behind the woods up to our left and would circle back about the time we reached the house. On gray late afternoons like this one, it is an unspoken habit to stop and sit on the edge of the porch for a few minutes. Time enough to scratch a good dog's ear, get a drink from the well, or catch a few deep breaths of cold, pine-scented air. Meg knows this, and she was waiting as we crossed the dirt path.

Something, however, wasn't exactly right. Meg turned suddenly and began to inspect the brush alongside the house, then came to a tentative stop looking under the porch. It was a sort of point, uncertain and uncharacteristic. In a young dog, you would immediately think terrapin or rabbit or snowbirds, and that is what crossed Mike's mind in that instant before reason said otherwise.

"Go on, Meg," he said, urging a decision. Scott and I

paused far too nonchalantly, our shotguns cradled in our arms. Unlike Mike, we are accustomed to hunting with dogs that take a more democratic approach to various wildlife.

"Go on, now," he said again, a bit more firmly. Meg's stance said that she found this just as incredible as we might, yet there was all this unlikely evidence wafting to nose right here under these sagging boards. She took a step and stiffened tail high, but it was too late. We had failed her. There was a muffled rattling underneath, and the covey—ten or twelve birds—blew out in a roar from under the end of the porch. Slack-jawed in disbelief, we watched them go in a tight pattern like pellets from a giant gun barrel.

Mike tossed his cap on the ground in self-disgust. He seldom makes that kind of mistake; his dogs almost never do, and wouldn't have then without our help. Yet there it was. Cardinal rule No. 1 — "Trust your dog" — in tatters. Still, we marveled. In all our combined years of bird hunting, we could not recall ever having found bobwhites under a house. But here were the roosts: pearly droppings in several piles where the birds had circled their wagons on previous evenings, backing up to one another for warmth and protection in their characteristic tail-in ring.

We consoled Mike while he apologized to Meg, but Meg was more keenly interested in setting matters right than in holding a grudge.

"They went down the edge of those woods at the head of the pond," said Scott. "Should be in or near that thicket."

We took our break and let the birds settle down. After all, they most likely had not scattered far, since no shots had been fired. With Meg ranging handsomely ahead of us, we spread out and entered the woods walking abreast, guns ready this time. A hundred yards deeper into the gloom, we began to find birds. Two on the ground ran through the undergrowth like Mohicans, then flushed beyond range. Another exploded head-high out of a tree after waiting until we had passed. Two others had also lit in trees, but instead of giving us a shot, they swooped to within inches of the ground and buzzed through brush like low-level night bombers. The others simply vanished, though I swore later I had seen one wearing a helmet peep out at me from a machine-gun bunker. The score was zip. We stood at the end of the woodlot in astonishment. Meg shrugged, but she knows more about birds than we ever will, as she had ably demonstrated earlier.

Mike just shook his head in admiration. "I don't think we have to worry too much about those birds. They've hidden under a porch, run when they should have flown, and lit in trees like no bobwhite Nash Buckingham ever knew. When they absolutely had to fly, we'd have done better hitting them with a sand wedge. I'd say that covey is well-adapted to survival."

This past spring, as I drove up to another old house near Estore's that I have renovated as a camp, I flushed a pair of quail. They were under my porch. In late July, I flushed their brood from under the same porch. They flew in a loose formation of about a dozen, wavering uncertainly on novice wings, looking for all the world like puffball recruits in newly assigned Spads.

I may not have to clean my gun all season.

Deerly Beloved, We Are Gathered

Dressed smartly in pink and green and trailing a backwash of Giorgio, the lady marched straight through the crowd to the fellow in the baseball cap.

"That your truck out there?" she asked, pointing past the shaded picnic tables to the field where the vehicles were baking in the sun. The truck, once dark blue, was caked with mud, and the rack in the window behind the seat held two scoped rifles and an umbrella.

"Yes'm, that blue one is" — he swallowed hard before adding — "mine." As he turned to answer her, we could read the message on his cap: "God, Guns & Guts."

"Uh oh," I whispered, nudging a companion, who was picking vanilla wafers out of his banana pudding. "I think we're about to witness a philosophical discussion."

"I believe I know you," she said to the young man. "You work for my husband, right?" He nodded uncertainly and looked at his feet as though he hoped to find a convenient hollow log alongside.

"Oh, I'm so pleased to see you again," she said with a smile as sincere as it was unexpected. "My husband tells me you're a deer hunter, and I just love deer meat. It's so good for you, isn't it? I'm told it has almost no cholesterol, and I just want you to know that if you have good luck this fall and wind up with a freezer full, I wish you'd keep us in mind."

An hour later, as people began to leave the annual company gathering, I noticed our acquaintance in the cap showing the lady and several of her friends which one of the many trees towering over the carefully mowed lawn had the best potential for a stand. They were getting along famously.

This may have been an isolated incident, but with white-tail populations at an all-time high and deer hunting more popular than ever, perhaps it's an encouraging sign that the sport is beginning to cut across social boundaries. It's now trendy to eat wild game, especially venison, and people are gearing up to hunt who never imagined they might do such a thing.

Consider the deer hunter from Sparta, Georgia, who chanced to fall in love — an affliction that's often near fatal to competing outdoor interests. That was no problem here. The couple exchanged vows sitting in a tree stand, both dressed in camouflage. The clincher is that this was the same stand where the new bride had killed her first deer the previous season.

The domestic front is not the only place where deer hunting's popularity is making news and gaining converts. Recently the General Motors truck assembly factory in Pontiac had to close its plants when only a handful of employees showed up for work on two consecutive days in mid-November. Plant managers did not think it was just a coincidence that these were the first two days of the Michigan deer season, but managers are paid to figure such things out.

"We approved as many vacations as we could, and we would have still been able to operate," said a spokesperson, "but unexcused absenteeism pushed us beyond the point where we could cover all the jobs. We need a better coping mechanism."

Maybe General Motors needs a better coping mechanism, but it sounds like the hunters are coping very well, thank you. Union officials pointed out that the Pontiac plant had a sizeable backlog of trucks, so apparently no harm was done. It was also revealed that forward-thinking management at a Volkswagen plant in Pennsylvania routinely declares a "deer day" holiday the Monday after Thanksgiving. What can you say about a major industry paralyzed by white-tailed deer? It's enough to make you proud to be an American.

Of course, having your favorite sport embraced by the masses has its disadvantages. Any serious trout fisherman will attest to that, since the sport of fly fishing has, for the moment, also become trendy. Models are wearing fishing vests in fashion magazines, and Wall Street warlords are taking their wives to Sun Valley for rainbows or Scandinavia for salmon. A few of these newcomers look vaguely fearful that they might catch something slimy, but so what? Most of them also seem to have a genuine interest in their newly adopted sport, and they also share a growing concern for our dwindling resources of woods and waters.

You could argue that it's better to have a crowded hunting or fishing spot than no spot at all. It's also better to be understood than to be under attack.

The truth is that some of this widening support may help save not only prime wildlife habitat but also the very sports it sustains. If so, we'll all benefit. If nothing else, there seems to be a slow realization that the sports of hunting and fishing — and particularly deer hunting — are at least in no danger of sliding down the tubes for lack of interest. Nor, with proper management, are the species sought by sportsmen in danger.

If fears of cholesterol, heart disease, and obesity are playing a small part in bringing some disparate elements together, that's encouraging. As the boss's wife said, venison is good for you. The realization may soon follow that fishing for trout or sitting in a deer stand is also good for you — and, ironically, good for trout and deer too.

Real Ducks, Fake Ducks

For the third time that morning, there were ducks looking at our decoys. We sat tensely, heads down, leaving the inevitable drip on the end of the nose unwiped until it hung like a bare light bulb. The flight, six or eight birds, swung across the point from our right, skirted the misty line of outside cypress, and headed directly toward us. Then, just out of range, their resolve seemed to falter. They didn't actually flare, but seemed to slip away discreetly like ladies excusing themselves to the powder room. Moments later, they were a smudge of black in the distance, heading rapidly away.

"They couldn't have seen us that time," said my son, Scott. "We were absolutely still. Do you suppose there's something wrong with our decoys?"

We stood and looked at the set, trying to picture it as a duck might. What could be wrong? After all, we had carefully made most of the decoys of juniper and basswood the previous summer. They looked great to us, but we were certainly prejudiced by the time and money we'd poured into them. Yet surely, we thought, a proper duck would stop to admire our carving skill rather than visit some miserable molded plastic or rubber fakes.

Nor could we blame it on the weather. The temperature hovered in the teens, and a brisk wind rattled the dry reeds shielding the blind. Dawn had revealed a sullen sky and a lake almost entirely iced over. In other words, it was a perfect morning.

Two hours earlier, in the dark, we had laboriously chipped out a circle in the nearly inch-thick ice, sliding the loose plates under the unbroken sheet to open up a pothole of dark water where our decoys danced on the black wavelets. It looked so inviting that either of us, had we been ducks, would have readily pitched into the middle and preened our camouflage. But the real ducks weren't buying it. They were shopping, to be sure, but we had yet to see the color of their money.

Frustrated, we resorted to the old family ritual of passing the time by exchanging old and piteous duck jokes. "Will that be cash or charge?" the store owner asks the duck who has just bought some Chapstick. "Just put it on my bill," answers the duck. Or we posed waterfowl riddles: "Could a blind duck find a duck blind?" Yes, it does get old rather fast, even for us, and especially on a day when there seems to be no reason to have to resort to such foolishness. We don't ask much, just a visit and perhaps a shot. Even when ducks were more numerous, we had already begun to approach duck hunting more as an exercise in tradition than anything else. There have been too many seasons when ritual was the only reward.

We stood again and looked at the decoys. In the distance, ducks were still trading along the horizon, meaning we could possibly anticipate another chance as long as the weather held.

"I think I see the problem," I said, "and if it doesn't work, it will at least give us something to try. We may have too many decoys in that small pothole. Some species of ducks won't fly over sitting ducks to land, and they also need open landing spots. You couldn't cram a real duck in that pothole with a shoehorn."

We waded back through the floating shards, picked up a dozen of the decoys, and positioned six of the best in a curving line near one edge of the ice, leaving the rest of the pothole open like the deck of an aircraft carrier. From the vantage of the higher blind, we viewed our repairs.

"There's plenty of room now," Scott said. "I think we may be onto something here."

Thirty minutes elapsed, then a pair of scaup wheeled around the distant point to our right. They came straight at us for perhaps five hundred yards, never wavering, while our nerves knotted like the rubber band in a balsa airplane. When they set their wings confidently, we both missed easy shots.

A few minutes later, from the deep corner of the marsh, half a dozen widgeon slid over the trees. They were headed for the open lake when they apparently spotted their juniper brethren nestled in the cozy tub in front of us. They peeled off like dive bombers, buzzed us once, then lowered their landing gear. This time, we each managed to get one.

Several other times that morning, we had ducks over our decoys. Twice, they came from behind us and we didn't see them until too late. Another time, we inadvertently spooked an interested flock when we stood to stretch our legs. We also passed up a shot at a female mallard out of concern for the mallard's current low population.

But what had so instantaneously transformed our decoys from duck repellents to duck magnets? We considered the various possibilities. Naturally, we dismissed dumb luck, and we finally arrived at the likely answer. Was it possible that we had used our keenly developed waterfowling skills to identify a problem quickly and solve it in an exemplary manner? We voted on it. It passed unanimously. We will not entertain any sizeable body of past evidence to the contrary.

Greasy Burgers and Curb Service

I am so weak. Following a mid-December quail hunt at the farm, my son and I stopped to fill up at a Creedmoor service station that had a grill.

"Want anything to eat?" Scott asked as I filled the gas tank. I shook my head, but when he got back in the truck, I knew I was in trouble. His hot dog had soaked through its wrapper and smelled heavenly. Chili and slaw juice were dripping off his elbows by the time he'd polished off the dog and two hamburgers, and I had nearly run off the road twice just watching him.

"You want a bite?" he asked. No, I didn't want a bite. I wanted to go back and eat hot dogs and hamburgers until they were running out my ears. I managed to hold off for twenty-four hours, then at noon the following day, I slammed the door on a refrigerator full of health food and went looking for grease. A body — this body — can stand only so much clean living.

This would never have been a problem if Scott had been eating a dog or burger from McDonald's, Hardee's, Wendy's, or any other home of homogenized hamburgers. They're okay, but it takes a certain kind of hamburger to evoke true passion — one fried from a frozen start on a grill in a 1950s-vintage joint and hurriedly constructed using traditional ingredients that are peculiar to this part of the mid-South, and particularly eastern North Carolina. Let me describe one.

The burger is placed in a plain bun that has been steamed as soft as a baby's butt, then slathered with yellow mustard, chopped onions, chili (no beans), and minced, runny slaw. No substitutes. No exceptions, though it's permissible for a high school student anticipating a date within a week to eschew onions. Okay, rat cheese if you absolutely insist. The proper way to order a complete unit is "full dressed" or "all the way." The assembled burger is then wrapped in cheap waxed paper that will immediately become soaked with grease. The same ingredients apply to a hot dog, except the dog must be red enough to make you suspect that it was made from floor sweepings at the kind of meat-packing house that caused Upton Sinclair to go Commie.

If you are wondering if a charcoal- or flame-broiled burger can qualify, forget it. Same goes for ketchup, mayonnaise, pickles, relish, sauerkraut, sesame seed rolls, and any other such stuff. I'd never even heard of putting lettuce and tomato on a hamburger until I was in the army stationed on foreign soil (Maryland). For pity's sake, some places even put salad dressing on hamburgers! I hate to be provincial about this, but these are suspicious, imported practices. Travel outside this part of the South and try to get slaw or even chili on a hot dog or hamburger. You could be locked up for asking. Worse than that, lettuce and tomato have been allowed to fester here long enough for whippersnappers under thirty years old to think they belong. Oh, what's to become of us? Is no regional peculiarity safe from the melting pot?

In the days of our youth, Charlie Ogletree and I were collectors of vintage greasy burgers and dogs and the places that sold them. Just recently, we spent half an hour on long distance reminiscing about places we had frequented in the 1950s and 1960s. One of our favorites was the Da-Nite Diner in Bethel when it was in a tiny, standing-room-only, faded blue brick carbuncle on the side of Wynne's Chevrolet. Somehow every fishing trip we ever took carried us through Bethel. The Da-Nite is still open, but it's moved around the corner into more spacious digs.

Other spots we would go out of our way to visit included the Radio-View Drive-In in Little Washington, The Creamery in Wilson, Melvin's in Elizabethtown, Amos and Andy's in Durham, Darwin Water's Pure Station in Greenville, Ham's in Weldon, Zack's in Burlington, the Emerald Isle Pier grill, and many, many others that have slipped my mind. I apologize if your favorite isn't among them. Some are history, some have gone upscale (alas), and some are still in business virtually unchanged.

Charlie also reminded me that some of these establishments once offered true curb service, a very rare feature today. You never went inside. Someone would come to the car and take your order, then deliver it on a window tray.

The Second Street Lunch in our hometown of Roanoke Rapids never offered curb service, and it has occupied three locations on the same block in my memory, but it's still legendary for its dark, spicy chili and burgers. My mother used to accuse me of coming home mainly to eat there, and it's true that I have eaten as many as six Second Street hamburgers at a sitting. Among the other Roanoke Rapids hangouts I recall were Mobley's and Ray's — both long gone.

When I grew up and moved away, a new friend in a faraway state one day remarked to me that he "wasn't going to take me to raise."

I was dumbstruck. "You mean you've been to Ray's?" I asked. He looked at me like I was crazy. You see, for all those years I was growing up, when anyone had used that old colloquialism, I had always assumed they meant they weren't going to "take me to Ray's." Well, sure — it had the same general meaning, didn't it?

A Goose for Lemmie

Long before daybreak, we leave the warm lodge and crunch on frozen grass past a scraggly cedar strung with unlit lights. A short drive takes us to the frame building south of the causeway where other hunters have already gathered to draw for guides and blinds.

Standing apart, some of the guides joke among themselves, all seemingly dressed far too lightly for the cold — a couple of flannel shirts topped by an oilskin and hip boots turned down at the knee. Obese in wool, goose down, and chest waders, the rest of us look like grizzlies emerging from a den. Our frosty breath mingles with cigarette smoke and the drifting exhausts of trucks and cars.

In the backs of some of the trucks or behind fogged windows, huge Labradors and Chesapeakes stand quietly, ignoring us with professional disdain. Their eyes say, Don't even think about scratching behind our ears when there is work to be done. We have our orders; geese will be retrieved.

I am one of the hunters, feeling a bit awkward and out of place. It occurs to me that I would probably fit in better with the dogs than with either the hunters or the guides. So I merely watch, storing moments like random clips of old movie film. It seems odd that you can seldom dictate what you want to remember, nor do the bits of film you manage to preserve have much meaning for anyone else. The unedited portions are too brief, too isolated.

Headlights from the guide's dusty black Chevrolet carve a yellow slice along the dikes bordering Lake Mattamuskeet as he drives us to his blind. As we stack our shotguns and gear in the skiff for the short trip up the canal, the flashlight momentarily illuminates the heads of decoys coated with rime. Thin ice cracks and tinkles like a crystal chandelier as the guide, followed by his yellow Lab, sets out decoys in the shallow water around the blind. Out of the hollow night, the flutelike calls of waking Canadas begin as single notes and gather disharmony—an orchestra tuning. We shiver, but not from the cold.

The light comes so imperceptibly that you are first aware only that the stars can no longer be seen. Later, as the sun rises through the rim of distant trees and thin clouds, the sheet ice and glazed vegetation are instantly aflame. It is, I think, always the best of it, a moment so intense that you swear you will never sleep through another winter dawn. Even when you know such a clear morning is a likely omen of inferior hunting, you can hardly fault its beginning.

Our guide, Lemmie Cahoon, has little to say, but his reserve is natural, without the patronizing air often adopted for "sports." It is obvious that he is here because he wants to be—would be here even if we weren't—and that he takes pride in his blind, his dog, and his years of experience. More than that, he seems pleased to share this day with companions drawn by lot and common interest. Perhaps it is because he is older—he appears to be in his seventies—but he also seems to feel no compulsion to continually remind us that we are merely clients or to prove his superior skill. It is a fairly rare attribute, one we instinctively appreciate. In return, we tell him we have no unrealistic expectations.

By midmorning, it is apparent that it is going to be a slow day. Indeed, the only geese we have seen have been on the distant horizon, long wavering lines flying to the fields to feed. He scans the sky, occasionally leaving the blind to move decoys that have blown together or knock the ice off their bills.

As the end of legal shooting approaches, he tells us of other hunts, of his early years as a waterfowler. Yet still he watches, and several times he expertly calls in ducks, most of which we miss. "No matter," he consoles. "You'll get 'em next time."

The geese slip in quietly, coming in low over the trees behind us — an improbable dozen returning early from the fields, uncharacteristically quiet. But Lemmie has seen them, almost too late, and his warning freezes us in awkward positions, a hand reaching for peanuts, a cup of coffee at chin level, a laugh riveted. Lemmie is in a crouch, and we watch his eyes to mark the approach.

"Behind us," he says. "Get 'em, boys."

Wings set, they are strung out above the marsh like a scene on a Christmas card. We each drop one, and the yellow Lab is instantly among them. Lemmie shares our excitement so convincingly that it could have been his first goose, too.

The year was 1959. Lemmie and my grandfather are long dead, but my father and a brother still share this memory, the kindness and the camaraderie of the best guide we ever hunted with.

This is for you, Lemmie.

A Jetty Too Far

A brisk northeasterly wind whipped a stinging spray off the crests of the waves, and even in the predawn darkness, we could see the long, white rollers washing over the narrow jetty at the southern tip of Wrightsville Beach. Tom Cooper and Andy Aretakis were far more excited about the prospects of walking out on that dark, slippery wall of cinderblocks in midwinter than I was, even if there were, as promised, big spotted sea trout feeding in the deep water that flowed through the inlet along the south side of the jetty.

It was cold, and the heavy wool sweater, rain jacket, and chest waders seemed to offer no more warmth than a pair of shorts and a T-shirt, although they certainly weighed enough to make the possibilities of an untimely swim seem foolhardy. Furthermore, the four cups of strong coffee I'd just swilled at an all-night establishment on the causeway had made me as jumpy as a dirt road lizard.

"I don't like the looks of this," I said as plug rods were jointed and lures tied on.

"Just take it slow and you'll be all right," Andy replied. "If you fall off, try to fall on the left side where the waves are breaking. It's shallow enough to stand there. The other side is deeper — about forty feet, I think."

Andy showed me how to pass someone on the jetty should the need arise. Since the wall appeared to be only about as wide as the length of my booted foot, two anglers passing would have to grasp one another like long-lost lovers and pirouette. It was not an encouraging bit of instruction.

Moments later, Andy and Tom were gone, and I could hear them laughing in the blackness as they shuffled seaward.

Oh well, I thought, it won't be the first stupid thing I've done in a lifelong quest for fish. Cradling my rod and reel, I stepped onto the jetty and began to inch my way out. The top of the jetty was covered with greasy algae, requiring careful placement of each foot. Waves broke over the top at intervals, but I managed to travel what seemed to be several miles — actually only about fifty yards — until I realized that someone was ahead of me on the jetty. Andy and Tom had already passed the unknown angler and were halfway to Portugal. Beyond him, I could see bigger waves pouring over the wall.

As I contemplated passing him, a wave broke underfoot and lifted me off the wall. For a terrifying moment I was waterborne, then the wave passed, setting me back atop the wall. This looks like a pretty good spot, I decided.

A pale light had begun to filter through the gray, scudding clouds by the time it occurred to me that I might do something besides stand there and watch for incoming waves.

Cautiously, I cast my MirrOlure into the inlet and began to retrieve it. After several casts, I began to feel more confident. This isn't too bad, I thought. Then I had a strike, but instead of a trout, it turned out to be a small bluefish that had virtually engulfed the MirrOlure. The hooks were so firmly embedded that I rammed my thumb through the gills from the rear to hold the blue's mouth open and work the hooks loose. Just as the lure came free, my thumb slipped forward and the blue gulped convulsively.

How can it be, I considered, that I find myself freezing at dawn in midwinter perched on a slick razor of concrete with the tip of my thumb protruding from the mouth of a dying bluefish that has clamped two rows of sharp teeth all the way to my knucklebone?

"Catch one?" asked the angler a dozen feet beyond me.

"Yeah, sort of," I answered as I literally tore the head off the bluefish and extracted my thumb. My arm was bloody to the elbow. Most of the blood was mine. I tossed the blue into the inlet.

"You're not keeping them?" asked the surprised angler.

"Nah, he's too small," I answered casually. I feigned an exaggerated yawn and tried to look bored. "Looks like there's nothing around today but these little blues. I think I'll take a break."

"Yep, it's pretty dull out here this morning," replied the angler.

I began to inch my way back to the beach, pausing at intervals and looking around with what I hoped would appear to be a reluctance to leave such a lovely panorama. The beach, now fully visible in the growing light, seemed to be several light-years away.

When I finally stepped off the wall onto the sand, I borrowed a none-too-clean towel from a surf fisherman and wiped off most of the blood. The look he gave me when I handed it back was exactly the look I would have given someone who had just thrown up in my living room.

"Why didn't you join us?" asked Andy when he and Tom finally came in and found me sitting on the beach.

"I did go out a pretty good ways, but all I could catch was bluefish," I replied. "How did you two do?"

"Not even a strike," said Tom. "We'll try them again later. Say, what happened to your hand?"

"My hand?" I answered, looking at it as though I was noticing it for the first time. "I must have snagged it on something. No problem."

Postscript: No, I did not go out on the jetty again. I will never go out on that jetty again in any season. All fishermen are crazy, but not all fishermen are that crazy.

File under Diversions

This is the time of year when most fishermen who don't also hunt are reduced to the peripheral pleasures of their sport, which, in most cases, boils down to achieving professional status as a couch potato and causing co-inhabitants to actively consider suicide or, more likely, murder.

There is a persistent myth that this is also the time to repair equipment. Outdoor columns are full of tips under the ubiquitous title "It's Tackle Tinkering Time," a topic apparently chosen for the same reason I have chosen it — there is nothing else to write about.

I confess I have little first-hand knowledge of any benefits or pitfalls facing tinkerers, although I did once hear of a fellow who shot himself cleaning his bow and arrows. However, in the interest of science, I wanted to see what I was missing, and first I set about to determine exactly what constitutes tinkering. The dictionary gave me this definition: "to busy oneself futilely with a thing; to work unskillfully or clumsily at anything." I can handle that, I figured. The second task was to decide what needed tinkering with most. Why not grease my fly lines, I thought, so that I won't have this task to do next spring?

I pulled out all my fly reels and began to strip off the lines and seek some way of stringing them out. Each line is ninety feet long, so it quickly became apparent that this is one of those tasks best done outdoors — where, of course, it was raining. Not to worry. I looped the end of a line to a chair in the living room, then walked through the hall, a bedroom, and the kitchen, arriving at the end of the line, so to speak, approximately back in the middle of the living room, where I tied it off on the leg of the coffee table. Six lines later, the house was beginning to resemble a giant spiderweb, with me and the coffee table fixed more or less permanently in the center. With some difficulty, I was able to negotiate my original passage and get all the lines (and myself) well greased.

Encouraged by this success, I decided to repair several small leaks in my waders. As every angler knows, holes in waders are invisible, even though they have the same capacity to transfer icy water as a six-inch pipe. I thought, Why not hang the waders by their suspenders on a nail in the basement, then fill them with water? I could easily spot the leaks and mark them with a piece of chalk.

I found a convenient nail and carefully checked the suspenders to make sure they would support the weight once the waders were filled. A garden hose served admirably to fill them. I was standing there watching the telltale spurts of water and congratulating myself on the wisdom of checking the strength of the suspenders when the nail pulled out of the wall. No doubt wader manufacturers prosper from such calamities, and my check for a new pair is in the mail.

In all the tinkering columns I have read, there is an enthusiastic recommendation that you clean out your tackle box, removing all items that you don't use. This is simple enough, though it wrongly assumes that you have only one tackle box. I spread newspapers on the living room floor and dumped out the contents of my boxes, making a mental note never to do that again. All lures have hooks and all hooks are efficiently designed, thus all 473 lures were immediately joined. Several tedious hours later, they were separated, although some took advantage of my momentary inattention to reattach themselves to their neighbors. It was like trying to enforce voluntary birth control in a rabbit hutch.

I replaced the lures and other various items in the box, considering the merits of each and discarding the worn-out or unnecessary gear in a large plastic trash bag. When the tackle boxes were again full, I carried the bag to the trash. In it were two pipe cleaners and a split shot.

My outboard motor was my next tinker target. I do not actually know what "winterizing" means, but it is the term tinkering experts use. In the absence of any clear instructions, I simply disassembled it, spreading the parts on newspapers in the living room. (The basement was still a bit damp.) It is astonishing how much oil and gasoline there are inside an outboard motor. Also, be advised that newspapers do not soak up nearly as much oil and gas as, say, a rug.

Perhaps I went about this all wrong, but I think it is fair to say that pundits who write glowing columns about the joys of winter tackle tinkering should be rounded up, tied securely with fly lines, greased with motor oil, and left to squirm on a pile of treble-hooked bass lures.

Enough Is Not Enough

What is a reasonable amount of time to spend fishing? I know lots of anglers who manage to get on the water twice a week from spring through autumn and still hold a job, raise a family, and keep the lawn below the knees. Even if they never fish at all during half the year, that's still over fifty trips a year. Many avid fishermen, especially retirees, average a hundred trips annually, and I have two close friends who go fishing perhaps 150 times a year. Indeed, I have met anglers who claimed they fished somehow, somewhere, nearly every day. Some would consider that excessive.

One thing all these people have in common is the belief that they are not fishing as often as they'd like, and most are actively arranging their affairs so that they can increase their time on the water at some point in the future.

I personally think I could make do with a hundred trips a year if I were careful not to squander too much of the allotment on low-percentage ventures during the off-season. You see, that's the problem. Obsession does not calculate in advance the number of trips canceled or impaired due to poor weather, equipment failure, less than optimum water conditions, uncooperative fish, injuries, unavoidable obligational interferences, various acts of God, or marriages and funerals (especially your own).

If you factor these into the equation — and all fishermen are constantly factoring — then an average of fifty to a hundred trips per year falls into more proper perspective. Weeks and months can pass with failure of one kind or another stalking you trip after trip.

I can sense the words that are forming on your lips. Poor baby. Only gets to fish a fourth of his waking hours, and has the audacity to whine about it. Well, yes. I can't whine for every fisherman or fisherwoman, but I suspect my experience is somewhat typical. If you love something, and you have high standards, you quickly realize that there is an inverse relationship between effort expended and dream fulfilled. How many holes-in-one can the average golfer anticipate in a lifetime? How many athletes make it to the Olympics, and how many of those win medals? How often, for heaven's sake, can even a lowly couch potato expect to achieve just the right combination of sofa, junk food, and trash TV?

I calculate that last year I made quests for hickory shad, white bass/striper hybrids, dolphin, Spanish mackerel, king mackerel, and flounder without catching a fish. The shad and hybrids simply didn't appear when they were supposed to. The dolphin inexplicably refused to eat and simply stared at us from the cobalt Gulf Stream. I spent three weekends casting from a pier for Spanish mackerel and had only two strikes. My king rigs haven't felt a strike in years. Had I caught a flounder, it would've been a fluke, and on one occasion I fed six dollars' worth of fresh shrimp to seagulls because my bait failed to entice a single sea mullet, spot, croaker, or pompano.

Closer to home, last year's warm winter and quixotic spring scrambled the bass and bluegill spawning patterns, and fishing remained erratic well into early summer. With one or two exceptions, the occasionally good big-lake bass fishing enjoyed by some of my friends took place while yours truly was otherwise engaged. A drought sucked many of my favorite ponds into the tobacco fields and crippled four months of late summer and fall mountain trout fishing. In other words, it was a very normal year, fishingwise.

That is not to say, however, that my obsession went entirely without nourishment. There is more to fishing than catching fish. It is often rewarding simply to get outside, and T-shirt philosophers have accurately noted that a poor day fishing is better than a good day working. Furthermore, some trips are salvaged by handsome surroundings, good camaraderie, or joyous solitude. Others are enriched by a touch of wilderness, a unique encounter with wildlife (but not too unique), or fine weather that lifts the spirits. All of these tend to become overrated if no fish whatever are caught.

But the key ingredients often turn on very small matters. Jack Avent and I actually caught quite a few largemouth bass last year, yet simply reducing fish to possession is not enough. More important is the manner of reducing, and we dearly wanted to catch those bass on topwater lures. The bass wouldn't hear of it. Who knows why?

Looking back over the year, I calculate that I had but one truly perfect fishing trip. It took place on a rainy summer day when I caught only one trout—a large, wild brown that I had been trying to catch for over two years. On that gray afternoon, I put months of careful scheming to the test. Two weeks earlier, I had even cut a rhododendron limb that threatened my backcast. I crawled within casting range, made one cast, caught the trout, photographed it, and released it. After it swam away, I sat on a rock for an hour in a steady downpour, measuring that transcendent moment against all the many outings that had been merely satisfactory, or less.

One truly memorable fishing trip a year may be enough. But only if you get a hundred opportunities.

The Best We Can Hope For

We all have a place we call home. The man and his wife sat in the living room in front of a gas log fire and told me about theirs. He could no longer walk without help, and although I didn't ask, it seemed clear it was his lingering illness rather than advanced age. His wife brought us coffee, then showed me around the house. It was a fine house in a large midstate city, home to them for more than fifty years. Yet it was not the home they remembered or wanted to talk about.

"It's gone now," he said, "or at least it's changed in ways that I never thought I'd see. Never wanted to see. Sometimes I get to thinking about it and I'm damn sorry I lived so long."

His wife took a sip of coffee, but her expression registered no surprise.

"There was this cabin beside a small stream back up in the mountains where we used to go right after we got married," he said. "Gee, it was a swell place. Darn near impossible to get to. No interstate highways then. It took us all day just to get to the foothills, then it was dirt road for another thirty-five miles, and finally not much more than a bunch of pig tracks. We'd park and carry our stuff the last mile around the side of the mountain to get to the cabin."

"No electricity, no water except the spring and the creek, no heat except the fireplaces," added his wife. "We'd go up in early spring when the wildflowers were just peeking out and the trees had that pale green look they get when the leaves are the size of a squirrel's foot."

"At night we'd sit on the porch, and you could see every star in the sky," he said. "There weren't no lights anywhere, and nobody else within miles. I liked to fish, and we'd hike up the creek and never see another soul or even a footprint. The trout were all 'speckles' — you'd call them brook trout now, and I guess that's what they really are. Natives, remnants of the Ice Age, with no inbreeding from stocked fish. You could drink out of that stream, and we did. Also skinny-dipped."

His wife smiled. "But only in the summer, and even then the water was cold," she said. "I don't think that water ever got more than about 50 degrees at the most. In order to have hot water, I'd keep a large pot sitting on the woodstove all the time. My friends back home would have thought I was crazy to enjoy such a place, but I believe we could have lived there year-round if Pappy hadn't had to work and we hadn't had kids to raise."

"The walks were the best part," he reflected, and his wife nodded in agreement. "We hiked those hills and streams for years and never even came close to seeing it all or getting tired of it. Some of the timber had been cut many years earlier, but it had grown back pretty good, and there was still right smart of virgin timber. We saw the chestnuts die. That was a sad thing. One steep cove was full of poplars and hemlocks that were so big that several people couldn't reach their arms around them. You couldn't see the tops, even at high noon; it was practically dark in there except for shafts of sunlight that filtered through sort of hazy and blue. Every rock was covered with deep moss. We'd go up there and just sit for hours and never say a word."

They were silent for a few minutes, and I sat there sipping coffee and thinking about places I had known that had meant a lot to me. I knew the answer to my next question, but I asked it anyway. "What happened to it?"

"Cabin's still there, I think, though we haven't seen it in right many years," he said. "You can drive to it easily now on a good logging road. There was an old mountain road that crossed the headwaters of the stream, and when they renovated it, the silt ruined the stream and killed all the native trout. It was restocked, but it never really recovered. Some of the areas — including that cove full of virgin timber — were cut. Not all at once, but over the years. After the logging road was put in, there were a lot of break-ins at the cabin. We finally started locking it, but that didn't do no good. Some of it was just vandalism; just meanness."

"It was shameful the way so many people left litter along the trails and the streams," said the wife. "And the last year we went up there, the motorbikers had taken over the trails. Of course, we couldn't walk the trails as well, because we were getting on in years, but we didn't want to see the way it had changed anyway."

I told them about what had happened to one of my favorite places on the Little Alligator River, and about another place on the Pamlico River where I'd spent some fine summers as a teenager. Both gone. And I thought of my own mountain hideout. Though it had changed little, it seemed suddenly vulnerable.

"You know," said the old man, "the strange thing is that I don't really know who to blame. The road that ruined that stream was needed, or so we were told at the time. Same for the timber. We didn't like what was happening, but it seemed selfish or hopeless for us to fight it. All I know is that it's gone, and it seems priceless to me now. Not a day goes by we don't think about it. I couldn't stand to go back and see it the way it is."

"Sometimes I think it's unfortunate that we ever had such a place," said the wife. "Our sons have their own interests — different from ours — and maybe they won't have to suffer such a loss."

But they will, I thought, and she knows it. Only a few of us—the very lucky, or perhaps the very stupid—live a lifetime without such losses. The last frontiers are rapidly disappearing; the forgotten corners are being swept up. And maybe the best we can hope for is that we will not outlive our dreams.

Where the Wind Comes From

Some years back, two boys about eight years old wrapped a double handful of cookies in tinfoil, cut two walking sticks out of a ligustrum hedge, and walked up the street to a culvert where a small creek flowed. They followed the creek upstream through backyards and a city park. In the pools, the water was murky, but where it ran over pebbles, it seemed clear. After walking perhaps half a mile, the boys entered a wooded area and lost sight of the houses. Tall reeds and dense brush shrouded the creek, filtering out the sound of traffic, barking dogs, and mothers calling their children home to supper.

At a spot where the creek tumbled over a series of bedrock ledges, they sat down and looked around. This is it, they figured. We're in the wilderness. They ate their oatmeal cookies and drank out of the most polluted creek in Raleigh.

After I realized that my son and his friend were not going to die of typhoid or something worse, I began to appreciate what they had done. I remembered a boy about their same age many years earlier who had decided not to go straight home from the swimming pool one summer afternoon. Instead, he followed a ditch for about a mile and wound up on the moon.

At least that's what I thought it looked like. Actually, it was a huge expanse of waste pine bark that covered many acres of lowland near the Roanoke River below a pulp mill on the outskirts of town. There were deeply cut trails through the chips, and in one place I found a cave in a shelf of pine bark. I walked that maze half believing that no one had ever been there before. And on the way home, I drank some of the oily water from the ditch. (I had a better sense of ritual than plain good sense.)

Sooner or later all kids get that first taste of exploration, and it usually taps a lifelong wellspring — an insistent need to go beyond what is known. That current flowed again recently while I was reading A. B. Guthrie's *The Way West*, a fictionalized but accurate account of the first wagon trains to travel from Independence, Missouri, to Oregon.

At one point a trapper who had first traveled west in the 1830s described his feelings upon seeing the same country again as a wagon-train pilot in 1845. Even that early, he was beginning to feel boxed in. The trapper "sat his horse and watched thinking how things had changed. This country was young, like himself, without the thought of age. There wasn't a post on it then, nor any tame squaw begging calico, but only buffalo and beaver and the long grass waving in the Laramie bottoms. The wind had blown lonesome, the sound of emptiness in it, the breath of far-off places where no white foot had stepped. A man snuggling in his robe had felt alone and strong and good, telling himself he would see where the wind came from."

Kids drinking from the polluted creeks over a century later were "seeing where the wind came from," and although it is a sad comparison, it can only become sadder. In just the past few decades, those of us who care about such things have suffered a steady and relentless loss. Many of the swamps and brackish backwaters I loved as a kid down east are gone, the rivers choked with algae. In the mountains, we exult in stolen moments of solitude, knowing full well that just beyond the ridge the bulldozers are at work. Those places not already accorded wilderness status or something similar are being mopped up, and there is pressure to unlock some of the meager wild country we've set aside.

There will be no more Oregon Trails on this planet, although there will certainly be some to other galaxies. It's our nature to seek them — and, alas, often to leave a trail of destruction.

Maybe that's the best reason of all to lock up what remains of our scattered wilderness on earth. Few of us will explore the vast cosmos, but we can visit the remaining fragments of frontier here and preserve at least the spirit of exploration. And we can do it without the stigma of destruction that accompanied the actual exploration undertaken by our forefathers. It is a substitute at best, but one many of us truly need.

Thoreau wrote, "In wildness is the preservation of the world." He was speaking of more than just the resource.

Cutting the Tree

If you want a Christmas tree this year, you'll probably go to one of many lots where commercially grown trees are staked out and tagged. You'll pick one out, pay for it, cram it in the trunk or tie it on the roof, and take it home. Actually, it's a nice little family tradition, and kids of all ages enjoy looking over the various trees until they find the one they want. The lots offer a wider choice of both sizes and kinds of trees than ever, and the tree you pick is likely to be far handsomer than any you could buy or find a decade ago.

This is a fairly recent development in North Carolina. It hasn't been so many years ago that if you wanted a tree, you had only a few choices. In the relatively small eastern North Carolina town where I grew up, you could run down to the neighborhood grocery and check out the red cedars leaning against the side of the building. A big tree might set you back $4.00, but you could get a pretty good one for $1.25. If you were interested in exotics, there might be a few scraggly blue spruce that consisted of a trunk and about four limbs, some of which still had a few needles clinging stubbornly to the tips. Spruces were usually more expensive than cedars, but I never understood why.

The other alternative — the one that most people chose — was to take the family on an afternoon drive in the country and find a tree. Even if you didn't know a farmer who would let you look for a tree, there was plenty of unposted woodland around where no one cared if you cut a cedar. I don't need to tell you that's not the case anymore, and few families still prowl the fields and wood-lands to find a wild tree.

Nostalgia may be the rust of memory, but even if my recollections of the annual family tree-cutting trip are flawed, it was still an exciting event for a kid. I can recall running through the woods and the overgrown fields hoping to be the first to find the perfect tree. There was more than a little competition between me and my broth-ers, Graham and John, and we quickly learned that the best cedars—full-bodied and bright green—usually grew in the edges of fields, and especially along hedgerows or fences. I didn't know it then, but the seeds are eaten by birds and are "planted" with the droppings that accumu-late when the birds light on the fences, power lines, or hedgerows. That's why cedars often grow in straight lines, as though a farmer had planted them.

Seldom did we find a truly perfect tree. Some were too tall, others too brown, and many had only one good side. But sooner or later, a decision would be made. Dad would saw it down, and we'd help drag it back to the car while the heady scent of cedar fueled our already-rampant Christmas spirit. (Mine was usually so rampant that by the time Christmas Eve arrived, I was running a fever, but Mom couldn't have gotten me to sleep with half a gallon of paregoric.)

Christmas is a very personal thing, and everyone has his or her own little traditions. Furthermore, I know that a Fraser fir is probably the most classic of all trees, and we've decorated some lovely ones. And yet, for me the only real Christmas tree is a cedar. Nothing smells better than a cedar. I don't care that you have to wear gloves to put it up. I don't care if it drops every needle two days after it's up. So what if the tip is too light to properly support a star? Cedars are Christmas trees.

And while I'm warming to the subject, I might as well

admit another lapse in taste. All these little white lights are beautiful, but every house in every neighborhood looks just exactly alike. Shucks, you can ride through entire neighborhoods without seeing a tree with colored lights — big, old-fashioned colored lights like a proper eastern North Carolina red cedar ought to have.

I may never cut another wild cedar, but something in my blood still stirs when I see a really good one while I'm driving down a two-lane blacktop. And Christmas is never more real for me than when I can look across a bleak December field and see a distant farmhouse with a string of colored lights draped out front on a bush, and a peaked row of blue lights in each window.

I think these are the colors of hope, but I could be wrong. And I really don't hold it against you if you've got a fir and white lights. There's no such thing as bad taste at Christmas.

A Different Kind of New Year's

Gusts of cold rain battered the truck for the first three hours before the windshield wipers began to pile up ridges of sleet. A few miles farther it seemed as though I had passed through the sound barrier into utter silence. The gusts and rattling sleet were replaced by a soft, fine snow falling out of a luminous gray sky. The clouds seemed very close and intimate, like old flannel blankets you could pull around your neck. As the snow began to cover the road, I pulled off and locked in the hubs on the front wheels of my old Bronco.

It was so absolutely quiet that I could hear the tick of tiny flakes on top of the truck and on the split rails of a fence that bordered the road. I stood for a moment and watched the rolling fields and distant foothills fade — a painting being scrubbed to white canvas. At that moment I knew I had made the right decision. New Year's alone.

It had been one of those last-minute notions. Facing a traditional celebration with tipsy crowds followed by football on TV and snoozing between snacks, I decided I'd rather plant one foot in the last century for a few days. As soon as that was settled, I knew exactly where to do it.

I passed fewer and fewer cars as the road became more treacherous, and by the time I turned off on the last fifteen-mile stretch of single-lane logging road, I was leaving the only tracks. I punched in a tape of Christmas carols and poured a cup of coffee from the Thermos. An almost delirious happiness took hold, and I was adding a superb bluegrass tenor — my judgment, of course — to "The First Noel" as I plowed through the last drifts to the cabin perched on the side of the mountain, overlooking the creek. Its three rooms are not much bigger than a chicken coop, and a fourth room sits twenty-five yards up the slope, its wooden seat cold and forbidding. With any luck, it would not be needed. I'm told the cabin was built largely from scrap narrow-gauge railroad ties scattered by the 1940 flood. As a summer trout camp, it's adequate, but it's hardly the shelter you'd pick in a blizzard.

Kitchen conveniences are limited to a portable two-burner stove, a toaster oven, and springwater piped into an old sink. Musty wool army blankets are piled on a bed in the tiny bedroom, and the living room barely holds a sagging cot, a decrepit armchair, a ramshackle table, and an oil lamp. There's electricity, but it's fragile.

You can see fire through gaps in the warped iron plates of the woodstove, and it draws so heartily it'll spin the damper, threatening to suck the burning logs up the chimney. From a cold start, it can radiate a cozy 120 degrees in ten minutes and have you basking in your drawers. But forty-five minutes later, you'll be looking for your sweater and fetching another chunk of wood.

While the cabin warmed, I stepped outside and tapped the thermometer (22 degrees), then crunched through the still-falling snow and cut some pine and hemlock boughs. Arranged on the table with a candlestick centerpiece, they began to release a fine seasonal aroma as I cut up beef and onions in an iron pot, then added peeled tomatoes, garlic, cumin, a bay leaf, cayenne, and chili powder. The traditional black-eyed peas (canned, alas) would go on the fire in a couple of hours, and the toaster oven would reheat the homemade apple pie I'd brought.

I cached the milk and oysters for tomorrow's stew in a snowdrift, swept a few shriveled critters out of the corners, and suddenly had nothing to do. I could go for a walk, read, perhaps take a nap, I thought. Or go fishing. Well, why not? I had brought my gear, though I couldn't say exactly why, and there would be plenty of time later for less active whims.

I did not actually expect to catch a fish, nor did it matter very much. Trout fishing does not require trout any more than virtue is always its own reward. I filled my creel with images of black water running swiftly under lacy edges of ice, midstream rocks sporting snow caps, and remnant berries glazed like tiny candied apples.

Winter anglers, even introspective ones, leave a curious trail. When your feet become numb from wading, you are persuaded that it will help to get out of the stream for a few moments. Very shortly, it occurs to you that the water, being still liquid, must surely be warmer than the snow, and you will wade back into the stream. You follow this circuitous route until you have one foot in the water and the other in the snow — both of them freezing — and the coffeepot starts calling.

Just before midnight, full of chili, peas, and pie, I walked up the road. The sky had cleared, and the stars sparked icy crystals. Somewhere, people were blowing noisemakers and keeping an eye on their designated drivers. Or perhaps there was no one left in the world. I could half believe it. And for one soul in one particular place on one New Year's, it was a world supremely at peace.